DEMON
PROPHECY

DEMON
PROPHECY

BY

JOSE ROMERO

CITIOFBOOKS, INC.
3736 Eubank NE Suite A1
Albuquerque, NM 87111-3579
www.citiofbooks.com
Hotline: 1 (877) 389-2759
Fax: 1 (505) 930-7244

Ordering Information:
Quantity sales. Special discounts are available on quantity purchases by corporations, associations, and others. For details, contact the publisher at the address above.

Printed in the United States of America.
ISBN-13:   Paperback   979-8-89391-053-7
               eBook   979-8-89391-054-4

Library of Congress Control Number: 2024907083

Contents

Fallujah Iraq

Turning the corner, we entered a broad street. A loud explosion filled the air. Sending my platoon scrambling for the nearest cover. Kneeling behind an abandoned orange and white taxi, myself and my Lt. felt small rocks and sand fall on us from above. The RPG had struck a building next to us.

"Dude, that was close!" Brad yelled. I turned to look at my Lieutenant. Sweat was pouring down his dust covered face. "Should we call for tank support?" he asked me.

"By the time they get here, it will be too late." I told him. "We need to move, have everyone push up, we can't get pinned down!"

Looking around, I could see the men in my unit. Using abandoned vehicles for cover they returned fire, with calm and controlled bursts. Brad shouted out my orders, the men moved into action. Their return fire increased, and one by one they moved up the street towards the insurgent positions.

I heard ak-47 rounds strike the old taxi we were behind. It was our turn to move. I spotted a small alleyway to my left. I took a deep breath.

"Bounding!" I yelled as I sprinted for the alleyway. I heard the rounds impacting around me, as I ran for my life. Making it in the alley, I positioned myself to

Give cover fire. With bullets hitting the pavement just behind him, Brad made it into the alley. He nearly knocked me over with his momentum.

The heat was intense, I could feel the sweat pouring down my face into my eyes, making them sting. It took a few seconds to find the next covered position to push to. We worked our way up the street, moving from one position to another. The whole time bullets flew around us. Looking through my scope, I could see the black shapes moving inside doorways and windows.

In a doorway I noticed a black shape, I watched as muzzle flashes appeared from the weapon he was holding. I lined the crosshairs of my scope on the figure, and squeezed the trigger of my m-4 twice. I watched as the black shape slumped and fell motionless to the ground.

Once we had moved to within 50 yards of the insurgent positions, the incoming fire stopped. It was how they fought, hitting us with RPG and small arms fire. Then once we got close they would just melt away. Leaving us to clear every building, one room at a time.

Reaching a large intersection, we took covered positions and paused to recon the area. I could hear the sound of humvees, making their way up the street we just secured. As they reached the intersection, I felt relief as they swung the 50 caliber machine guns down the streets.

"The Calvary is here." I told Brad. "We have Supporting

fire, let's push across the street." Just as The words left my mouth, an RPG flew right in front of us. It struck the lead humvee; a large explosion knocked me to the ground. I watched in horror as the vehicle became a large ball of flame. I felt so helpless as the fire burned. Anger built up inside me, four young men had just lost their lives. I felt a tug on my shoulder. It was my staff sergeant.

"Captain, the shot came from that building!" He yelled. He pointed to a three story stone building, across the street to our left.

"Let's get there before they get away." I said coldly.

"Ya dude, payback." Brad mumbled.

The staff sergeant called over the radio for support fire, as we advanced to the building. Forming a stack of nine, we rapidly crossed the street. Looking through the scope of my m-4, I saw no movement as we approached the target building.

"Send a team to cover the back, if they are still in there I don't want them getting away." I told the sergeant. Three men split from the stack and headed for the rear of the building. Reaching the front entrance, we set for a breach. The lead man noticed the door was slightly open. Quickly he threw a flash bang through the doorway. Just as the blast shook the room, we entered.

We entered a large room, each of us covering a portion of the room. Along the right side of the room was a large wooden counter. And in the center of the room were rows of metal folding chairs. The place appeared to be a large waiting room.

A large stair case filled the left side of the room. We headed up the stairs with caution. Reaching the second floor, we spread out covering the two doorways in the room. I signaled three men to clear the room to the left, and myself, the L.t. and sergeant to clear the room on the right. Reaching the door, I used a mirror to look into the small glass window. Inside I could make out a single bed and a small table. On the bed was what appeared to be a small boy tied to the bed frame.

"Clear." I heard the other team call out as they completed the search of the room they entered. I turned and signaled for them to proceed to the top floor. They nodded in response and headed up the stairs.

We entered the room; clearing the room we slowly approached the person on the bed. It was a small boy, maybe twelve years old. It appeared he had been tied up for a couple days. On the table by the bed was a burning candle, an open Koran and small wooden idols. What did they do to this child?

Was he being tortured for talking to Americans, or was he a hostage being held for some kind of ransom?

The leather straps used to tie him down had cut into his flesh. His lips were dry and cracked, and I noticed several scrapes and bruises on his face and arms.

"Call a medic, and get a translator." I ordered. The staff sergeant keyed his mike and made the call. "His pulse is very strong." Brad said with a hint of surprise in his voice.

He softly put the boys arm down, but stayed staring at him strange. I pulled my knife from my m.o.l.e vest and began to carefully cut the leather bonds. I looked at his face; I have a daughter his age I thought to myself. After cutting the last of his bonds, I walked over to the table close to the bed. The open book on the table had to be the Koran. I couldn't read the writing, but the book was highly decorated. Arabic writing was beautiful; too bad I couldn't read a word of it.

"Those are prayer rugs." Brad said, walking around them. I looked closely at the rugs; they were aligned east to west. That's normal, but what are prayer rugs, and a copy of the Koran doing in a torture room.

Muffled gunfire echoed through the building. We all tensed and looked up at the ceiling.

"Third floor clear." A voice said over the radio. "Two Insurgents down, proceeding to the roof."

"Solid copy, good job!" I answered. I let out a sigh of relief. "They got them." I said softly. Brad gave a big smile

"I think he's coming to." The sergeant called. Brad and I walked to the bed. The boys head moved. A deep moan came out of his moving lips, but his eyes remained closed.

"Don't be afraid." I said softly. "We are going to

help you." His head stopped moving. I leaned close to his face, and brushed his oily black hair back with my gloved fingers.

Suddenly his eyes flew open. I froze, my heart felt like it stopped! I was gazing into pure white eyes, no pupil's just solid white. I heard Brad suck in a big breath.

"What in the hell did they do to his eyes!" The sergeant exclaimed.

I turned my head breaking the gaze of those terrifying eyes. At that instant I felt a hand grab my vest. Next thing I knew I was flying backward through the air. I landed hard on the floor, sliding on the tile. Struggling to get back on my feet, I watched as Brad landed on the floor a few feet to my left. The sergeant lifted his m-4, but was knocked over as the boy struck him on the shoulder. With amazing speed this small boy jumped from the bed to the barred window. With the agility of a cat he was perched on the window sill facing us. Holding onto one of the bars with his right hand. He was motionless as he stared at us with those ungodly eyes.

Noisily we got to our feet. The three of us pointed our weapons at the boy. Three small red dots from our laser sights lit up his chest. This was the first time I ever sighted my weapon on a child.

A dangerous child I thought. How could this boy, no more than twelve years old and about ninety pounds, toss three grown men around like rag dolls? "Jesus Christ that boys strong." Brad said.

"There is no Jesus, no god!" The boy spoke in perfect English. His voice was odd. It was the voice of a young boy, yet a very deep and menacing voice spoke at the same time.

"Down on the ground!" the sergeant ordered. "Or I'll be forced to shoot!"

"What the hell is that?" Brad mumbled.

The boy's head turned, his eyes focused on Brad. A sly smile appeared on his lips. It looked out of place on the young boys face.

"Nephilim." The boy spoke in the strange double voice. "Down on the ground!" the sergeant repeated forcefully. The boy's gaze switched to the sergeant. Then he slowly looked down at the three red laser dots on his chest.

The boy leapt up. In less time than a heartbeat, he was crawling on the ceiling. He moved quickly across the ceiling. With every move pieces of plaster fell to the floor. His fingers and toes digging holes as he moved. Spider like he crawled faster than we could train our weapons. Three red dots followed him as he crossed. He stopped at the doorway, hanging over it. With a loud snap he turned his head till it was facing us. His head had turned so it was now facing backward.

"Oh my God!" Brad exclaimed. The three laser dots were now pointing at the middle of the boys back.

"Your god abandoned you, he will return and kill you." The boy spoke again "You live a lie!"

I heard steps, I looked at the doorway. The medic was approaching. The boy grabbed his helmet as he walked into the room. He lifted the medic off his feet in one swift move. One twist and this small boy could break the soldier's neck.

I had no choice left. I pulled the trigger twice. The room filled with gunshots. I could see the rounds hit their target. The three of us fired at the same time. The boy fell to the floor with a thud. The medic fell to his knees, the body of the boy lying in front of him.

"Are you ok?" I yelled to the stunned soldier.

"What the hell was that?" He replied.

Slowly we walked to the body, keeping our guns trained. The medic turned the boy's body over. His head was still facing backward. Gently the medic turned the boys head around, the sound of crunching bone shocked him. The boy's eyes opened. No longer white, the boys own brown eyes stared at the ceiling.

The boy mumbled something in Arabic. The only word I could understand was Allah. Then his eyes fixed and he was still.

I felt a lump in my throat. I put my head down. His last words were spoken with the voice of a boy. No other voice with it, just that of the boy.

"Dude, did that just happen?" Brad asked.

I looked at the ceiling; the marks where he had crawled were there. It took a couple of seconds to register what had just happened. I nodded yes in reply.

The battle for Fallujah ended two days later. We pulled out and returned to Baghdad, where we finished our tour.

Home

Leaning back the seat in the aircraft, I made myself more comfortable. Taking a deep breath I looked around. My unit was leaving Iraq. After a year we were going home. Everyone was so excited; you could feel the energy in the air. A young private was seated next to me. He seemed nervous, so I gave him a smile. He smiled back and seemed to relax a little. My thoughts drifted to my wife and children, I would soon be with. I couldn't wait to hug them and hold them close. I had skyped with my wife five days ago. I was so excited to tell her we were going home. She had an odd tone in her voice at the news. But plans change in the Army from one day to the next. Maybe she didn't want to get her hopes up yet.

The plane began to move and everyone fell silent. I could feel the plane accelerate down the runway. As we took off a loud cheer erupted. Reality finally hit us. Were going home!

The flight seemed to take forever. So I closed my eyes and drifted off to sleep. I was startled awake by the men cheering. I opened my eyes and saw them smiling and laughing with one another. I had just missed the announcement of our arrival. I could feel the plane turn, and we started our descent.

Excitement was in the air, all the hardships we had endured over these past months. Just seemed to melt away, nothing mattered anymore, we are home.

As the plane came to a stop, I stood up and made a short announcement to the unit.

"Gentlemen and Ladies, it was my honor and privilege to serve with you. I have never commanded a better group of soldiers. And I am proud of each and every one of you." I stated. "Now we have waited long enough for this moment. Enjoy and cherish every moment. We are home!"

With that being said everyone stood and excitedly headed for the exits.

As I walked into the terminal, I could hear screams. Children yelling "Daddy!" and crying as soldiers and loved ones greeted each other with hugs and kisses and lots of tears.

I looked around the terminal for my wife and children. I didn't see them, so I moved through the crowd looking for them. I expected to hear "Daddy!" and get tackled by my children, but nothing. I watched the soldiers and their families leave. Soon I was the only soldier left in the terminal.

"Maybe they are running late?" I thought to

myself. I pulled out the cell phone I took with me. It still worked. I dialed on my cell, but no answer not even a voice mail. One hour and five calls later, I decided to catch a cab home. Maybe they have their days mixed up.

The cab ride home felt like it took forever. As the taxi pulled up in front of my home, I eagerly got out and hurried to the door. I would surprise them I thought to myself. I quietly turned the doorknob, it was locked. I rang the doorbell, and stood back waiting to surprise whoever opened the door but no one answered. I put down my pack, and walked over to the potted plant where we always hid a spare key. I picked up the key and unlocked the front door.

My heart dropped, my pack thudded to the floor. I stood frozen in shock. I was staring into a nearly empty house. The once decorated walls were now bare. The living room, once filled with a large sectional sofa was now replaced with a small futon. The big screen television, end tables nearly everything was gone. All that remained was the futon, an old coffee table and a small television on a tiny table. I slowly walked to the table in front of the futon. On it was a large brown envelope and a letter with my name on it.

With trembling hands I picked up the letter. I

opened it and in my wife's handwriting it said.

"Dear Jose, I don't know how to say this but here it goes. You have been gone a long time, and things have changed. I have been alone to long, and have met someone who will always be there for me. I didn't want to tell you while you were there. You needed to focus on what you had to do to stay alive. I couldn't

Please don't come looking for me, I have made up my mind. The envelope contains divorce papers I filed. Please sign them. I am not asking for anything from you, not even child support. I will drop off the kids this weekend to see you. You can see them anytime you want. Please don't make this harder than what it is. I won't change my mind. I am in love, and plan to marry soon. I am so sorry things didn't work out, but you went here for me.

Debbie.

Tears filled my eyes. My legs started to shake, and I could feel my chest being ripped apart. I sat on the futon, and put my face in my hands and wept.

I lifted my head up, and looked around with stinging eyes. The room was getting dark, how long had I been sitting here?

I stood up and walked into the dinning room.

The oak dinning table was gone, replaced with an old card table and five metal chairs. Looks like they brought all the old stuff from the garage to replace what they took with them. At least it's something I thought.

I walked into the kitchen; next to the sink was a stack of paper cups. I filled one and drank the cold water with big gulps.

The house was quiet, too quiet. Slowly I walked around the house. Stopping to look into every room. They all were nearly empty.

I made my way to the garage, wiping the tears from my eyes I looked around. To my surprise almost everything I remember was still in there even my car. I went to the grey metal key box, opened it and found the keys still inside. I got them and put them in my pocket. At least I had a way to get around.

I went back into the kitchen and opened the fridge. There were lunch meats and a twelve pack of coke inside. I reached to open the coke box, and noticed a sticky note on the box. It said we love you dad, and it was signed by each of the kids. Again my eyes filled with tears. I had been craving a big greasy burger with green chili since Iraq. So I decided to go get one. I reached into my pocket and pulled out the car keys. I knew the perfect place; it was only a couple of blocks away. I opened the door to the 1997 Mitsubishi eclipse and put the key in the ignition. I turned the key and the engine roared to life. I gave a small smile at the sound the euro muffler gave. I opened the garage door and headed out.

That night I grabbed the blanket from what was once our bed. I didn't feel right sleeping there. So I took it to the futon. I fell asleep the moment my head hit the pillow.

The next morning I was woken by the doorbell. I got up and opened the door.

"Daddy!" I heard my kids yell. Before I could blink they tackled me. I held them all close, as tears of joy ran down my face.

We had a great weekend together, watching movies, eating pizza and shopping. I was feeling happy. When it came time for them to leave, my oldest daughter told me they wouldn't be coming next weekend. They were all going to six flags. I hugged them all tight and told them to have fun. My daughter told me to stay inside till they were gone. I figured she was right, that way there would be no problems. I hugged them close and told them I loved them with tears in my eyes. I stood in the middle of the room as they walked out and closed the door behind them. I felt both happy to see them, and torn to pieces watching them leave.

I had a choice to make. Do I retire, or do I stay in the army? I opened my pack and took out the folder containing my retirement request. It was submitted but wouldn't become final for thirty days. So I had plenty of time to cancel it and stay in.

I looked around the empty house. This wasn't the life I had dreamt of the whole year I was away. A life of being alone, growing old alone. I walked into the kitchen still holding the papers. I opened the lid to the garbage can and threw the papers into it. Well I made up my mind. I would stay in the army!

I was watching the news on TV, trying to catch up with what was going on in the world. My cell phone rang. I picked it up and Brads name was on the caller id.

"Hello." I answered.

"Hey cap, how's it going?" He asked me.

"Well not what I expected." I answered; I didn't want to unload my troubles on him.

"I know about it." Brad replied, shocking me. "Megan told me when I got home, I guess they had talked."

"Why didn't she say anything?" I said a bit irritated.

"She didn't want to worry us I guess." Brad said. "I am sorry man."

"It's not your fault." I said calming down. His voice was strangely reassuring.

"Ummm, Cap I need to ask you a huge favor." Brad asked nervous.

"Sure, what's up?" I answered.

"Could you come here, I really need your help?" His voice was almost begging.

"What's wrong?" I asked concerned.

"I will show you when you get here, you will come won't you?" He pleaded.

"Yes, sure I will leave in the morning." I said. "I don't have anything else to do."

"Really, dude that's great!" He said relieved.

"I'll drive; you're only like six hours away." I said. "Gives me a chance to blow the carbon out of the eclipse."

"I knew I could count on you." Brad said.

"Hey, you had my back in Iraq, it's the least I can do." I replied.

"Awesome, I will see you tomorrow then." He said.

"Give me your address so I can enter it into my gps." I asked.

I grabbed the pencil on the coffee table and wrote it down as he gave it to me.

"Thank you again." Brad said.

"Solid copy on that." I answered out of habit. The call ended and I put the cell down.

I spent the next hour packing what few things I had for the trip. There were no civilian clothes in my closet, so my acus would have to do. Why go buy civilian clothes when I would be back on duty soon.

After everything was packed, I loaded it all into the tiny trunk of the eclipse. I spent time in the garage checking all the fluids and belts on the car. I wanted to drive instead of flying. I needed time to think and absorb all that had happened, these past couple of days. I showered and went to sleep.

The morning came, and after three cups of coffee I was ready to leave. I locked up the house and set the gps to the address Brad had given me and drove off. After stopping for fuel and another cup of coffee, I headed out of the city. It was a warm sunny day. So at the last red light out, I pushed the button and put the top down. Putting in a cd of Beatrix Ramosaj I had in the car I turned the volume to max. Some teenage boys pulled up beside me at the light, they turned to look at me strangely. It was either the sight of an older man in uniform driving a white eclipse convertible, with checker flag designs on the side and eighteen inch rims. Or that I was blasting Albanian music.

I laughed slightly and pressed down on the gas hard, leaving them far behind.

I had driven about two hours. I felt hungry, but I still had about another hour and a half before the next city. I should have brought something to eat, I thought to myself. A few minutes later I saw a sign up ahead that read. Gas, food five miles. I reached the exit in no time, and turned off. I didn't see a town ahead, just a handful of small buildings and houses.

I pulled in front of the café. I stretched and

grabbed my wallet and got out. I needed a smoke. That's one thing you can't do driving seventy five miles per hour with the top down. After I was done I went inside.

It was a small place, but decorated nicely in the colors of Italy. It was very clean and whatever was cooking sure smelled great, my stomach growled.

An attractive young woman with long black hair came up to me.

"Hi there soldier!" She said politely. "Table for one?"

I smiled and nodded my head.

"Sit where you like, you have the place to yourself." She said with a cute smile. She motioned me to sit with a sweep of her am.

I chose a small booth in the corner.

"Can I get you something to drink?" She asked smiling.

I had served next to a British unit in Iraq, and loved the way they spoke. We would listen to them speak,

And after awhile we had gotten pretty good at imitating their accents. We would talk to each other often, phrases like bloody hell you sod and cheerio became normal for us. So I thought I would use it now.

"Yes Deary." I said with my British accent. "I would like to order a hamburger with cheese, some potato fries and a fizzy drink."

She looked at me strange for a moment. Then looked at my uniform. I smiled at her patiently.

"Sure she said, but one question what kind of fizzy drink would you like?" She said with an amazingly Good sounding British accent of her own.

"Just a coke." I replied in my normal voice, laughing hard.

She laughed and winked. "It will be out in a flash." She said as she walked away.

There was something magnetic about that girl. I pulled out my phone and looked at the time. I'm on schedule, no need to hurry. A few moments later she returned coke in hand.

"Here is your fizzy drink, Captain Romero." She said sweetly.

"How did you know my name?" I asked.

"It's on your uniform silly." She said. I felt dumb for asking.

"So how long have you been in the military?" She asked me.

"Twenty three and a half years." I replied.

"Wow!" She said amazed "Thank you for your service."

"Welcome." I said. I couldn't help but stare into her green eyes as she spoke.

"I don't get to talk to many people." She said, as she looked around the empty café. "If it wasn't for the locals we would have to close."

"A sign out on the highway would help." I said. "It would let people know you're here."

"I know but the fee for a billboard is to expensive." She said sadly.

"I bet you have been all over the world." She said changing the subject.

"Yes, quite a few places." I answered.

"I'm twenty five and never even left the state." She said, as she looked out the window.

"Really." I replied. "Why don't you travel?" "My family owns this place, and we make just make enough to get by." She said sadly.

Order up I heard a woman's voice say.

"Ill be right back." She said, and quickly walked away.

I had just met her a few moments ago, and I felt bad for her. I guess I'm not the only one with problems.

"Here you go soldier." She said, placing the food on the table. "Enjoy."

"Thank you." I said. She turned and walked away, disappearing through the door to the kitchen. The food was great. Even better than my favorite burger place back home.

Home I thought, its not home anymore. My reasons for being there are gone. If I retired now, I would always be alone. My children would visit me some weekends. Maybe I could get a nommal job to keep myself busy. But that's not the life I wanted, being alone. I guess my home from now on would be where ever the army told me to go.

I noticed the waitress come out to the dinning room with a small plate of food. Sitting down a few tables from me, she looked up at me and smiled. I felt sorry for her eating alone. So I put on my beret, picked up my plate and coke and walked over to where she was seated.

"Would you mind if I join you?" I asked her nervously. "No use us eating alone right?"

"Sure, I would love that!" She said smiling. I sat down nervous.

"I see you're single now." She said smiling. "I can see the ring mark on your finger."

"You don't miss a thing." I answered.

"That's why I am single." She laughed. "Guys can't lie to me."

"Well I have no intention of lying to you." I replied. "That's good, I would know." She smiled

She reached over and grabbed my hand. I felt a tingle go through me at her touch. She lifted my hand and touched where my ring once was, the discoloration quite obvious.

"Now what happened?" She asked.

I explained what happened, and she listened quietly. As we ate, we talked and laughed about other things. Things her customers would do or say. She asked about places I had seen, and told me the story of her life. We talked for over an hour. Our drinks were empty so I volunteered to get refills. I felt very comfortable, and at piece talking with her. Then she asked me what I was doing, way out in the middle of nowhere. It shocked me back to reality. I didn't want to go, but I knew I had to.

Lessia, I found out her name during our conversation, gathered up the plates and took them to the back. A few minutes she returned with the check. I gave her my credit card to pay for the meal. When she returned, she stood there for a moment. Writing something on the receipt, she folded it and handed it to me along with my card. I opened up my wallet, and pulled out a hundred dollar bill. I folded it quickly and placed it in her hand, as I closed her fingers around it at the same time.

"Thank you, I enjoyed lunch and your company was wonderful." I told her.

"Will you stop again soon?" She asked, staring into my eyes.

"You have my word." I told her. She smiled and I started walking to the door. I put the receipt in my pocket and put on my beret.

"Oh my god!" She said. "Thank you so much." I turned to see her holding the tip in shock.

"Your welcome." I told her as I left. I got into the car and started it up.

I glanced at the café and was surprised to see Lessia looking out the window at me. She smiled and waved, I waved back as I drove away. She was amazing I thought to myself, if only I was ten years younger. I put in a cd of Tiffany Page, a British singer as I sped down the road.

Day One

Thank god for gps, I thought to myself. The city Brad lived in was very confusing. It was a large city, nothing like New York but large none the less. The eclipse sped down the free way at sixty five miles per hour, I could see the tall buildings of downtown getting closer. I kept following the arrow on the gps. I listened carefully to the female Australian voice that told me when and where to turn. After passing the downtown buildings the voice told me to tum off. After a few more confusing streets, I reached a quiet looking neighborhood. The gps told me I had arrived; looking at the two story house I read the numbers above the door. They matched the address he gave me. I pulled into the driveway and shut the engine off.

I got out of the car and stretched. Lighting a cigarette I pulled out my phone. I was just about to send Brad a text saying, I'm here I think. When I heard his familiar voice.

"Hello Cap, how was your trip?" Brad said. I turned to see Brad walking quickly up to me. There was something different about him. His eyes seemed tired, and bloodshot. And his always peppy step was now tired and slow. He walked up to me and gave me a hug, slapping me on the back.

"I'm so glad you're here." He said. He asked me for a smoke and leaned on the eclipse.

"You still have it." He said, rubbing his hand on the

hood.

"Yes, it was still there waiting for me." I replied.

"Hey dude, I'm so sorry about that are you ok?" Brad asked.

"I'm ok." I said. "But I don't think you asked me here to talk about that."

"Come inside we need to talk." Brad said. I followed him down the walk to his front door. He looked at me and opened the door. I noticed right away that the house was chilly inside. It was dark; my eyes took a couple of seconds to adjust. The house was decorated in old fashioned wood furniture, with large paintings of towns on the wall. Megan must have been the decorator, Brad didn't seem like a decorator type.

"Megan, the cap is here." Brad called. I saw a door open and his wife came walking out. I had met her a few times before. In her hands she had two cups of coffee.

"How was your trip?" She asked.

"It was nice." I answered. She reached me and handed me one of the cups. "Thank you." I said to her. She smiled and sat at a large four seat table.

"Sit down cap." Brad said. I sat down and he sat across from me. Brad and Megan looked at each other in silence. The room was uncomfortably quite, so I decided to talk first.

"So what do you need my help with?" I asked. I could see the color drain from their faces, as they looked up at the staircase.

"Umm, Its Brandi some thing is wrong with her." Brad stuttered.

"Is she sick?" I asked concerned.

"The hospital couldn't find anything wrong with her." Megan answered.

"What does she have?" I asked.

"She got sick the day after I got back." Brad said. "What can I do to help?" I asked wondering. "I'm really not a doctor."

"You will understand once you see her." Brad said, giving me a strange look. He stood and motioned me to follow him. Megan got up also and walked behind us, a worried look on her face. As I followed Brad upstairs I was trying to figure out in my mind what could be wrong. And why they would need my help. We reached a small hallway, I followed him till we reached the doorway at the end. Brad got a weird look on his face as he reached for the doorknob. He slowly opened the door, and walked in. I slowly walked into the room.

Brandi was lying in the bed, she appeared to be sleeping. I noticed her face was very pale. Her long brown hair was covering half her face. Brad walked up to the the right side of the bed, and I stood behind him. Her closed eyes looked dark and sunken. Blankets were pulled up to her neck, only showing her face and hair. I am no doctor but she looked very sick. "The hospital didn't see anything wrong?" I asked, puzzled. One look at her and I could tell something was wrong.

"She changed when we got to the hospital." Megan said. "She was normal, and then when we got home she got sick like this again." I must have looked at them strange, because Brad answered me right away. "Let me show you." Brad said. He leaned over his daughter and gently shook her with one hand.

"Brandi, wake up sweetie." He said. I saw Brandi move under the covers, her head turned toward Brad as she opened her eyes.

"Oh my god!" I whispered. Every hair on my body stood up, and my body froze. My mind raced back to that day in Iraq. When that young boy opened his eyes. The same eyes that were now staring at Brad. Pure white cold, terrifying eyes.

Everything slowed, like watching a slow-motion movie. Megan began to cry, her eyes filling with tears. A look of both terror and worry for her child. Brad stood there motionless. My heart began to beat again. I took a step back, not wanting to be flung across the room this time. Brad looked at me with hope in is eyes. I guessed he thought I would have answers. Brandi slowly closed her eyes and began to whisper in a language, I didn't understand. She began moving her head slowly from side to side. Whispering the unknown words the whole time.

"She's been like this all night." Megan said sobbing.

"I haven't heard the language before have you?" Brad asked me.

I listened carefully to the words she spoke. I have been to many places in the world.

But I couldn't place the words. They didn't sound Arabic or Asian, Russian or European. I was at a loss; I looked at Brad and shook my head no.

Brandi opened her eyes, but this time they were normal. She started crying and called for her mother. In a heartbeat Megan was there beside her, holding her head in her lap.

"Mommy what's happening to me?" Brandi said, sounding exhausted.

"Everything will be okay," Megan said as she softly caressed her daughter's cheek, which seemed to calm her down. She closed her eyes and was fast asleep.

"We need to talk." I told Brad, motioning him outside the room. He looked at Megan worried.

"Its ok go, I'll be there in a moment." She told him. He smiled at her, and then followed me out of the room. We walked to the end of the hallway, and I stopped there.

"Now you see why I called you." Brad whispered to me

"It's like Fallujah." I said quietly. "We are going to need a lot of help. We need to find a way to help her, without hurting her."

"I know." Brad replied. "We are not shooting my daughter!"

Brad took me to his office he made in his basement. He had a computer and a laptop we could use, to look up information that might be useful. I used the laptop on the table.

I spent the next two hours, looking up everything I could find on demons and possession. So immersed was I in my search. I didn't notice the coffee and cookies Megan placed on the table next to me. I pushed my chair away and looked at Brad.

"There is not really much on how to combat this." I said rubbing my eyes.

"I didn't find anything really helpful either." Brad answered me.

"Why don't we call father Patrick?" Megan asked. "I'm sure he could help."

"It wouldn't hurt." I said shrugging my shoulders. "I'll do that now." Brad told her. He picked up his phone and searched for the number. Meanwhile there was something I had read, that I wanted to try.

"Megan, do you have a small cross?" I asked her. "Upstairs, I'll get it for you." She said. She hopped of the desk she was sitting on and went upstairs.

Brad was already on the phone, so I went upstairs. I met Megan in the upstairs hallway. She handed me a small metal crucifix. I looked at it for a moment. What was I getting myself into? I'm a soldier not a priest; I didn't have strong faith in religion. Even my dog tags read no religion. And now I'm going into the unknown. The army doesn't train us in spiritual combat. Well the one thing I learned in all my years in the military was, to watch the back of your buddies and they will watch yours. These are my friends, and I will do whatever it takes for them.

I walked over to Brandi's door and opened it quietly. She was asleep under the covers. Good I thought to myself. I walked slowly and quietly to the bedside. I got the cross and gently placed it on her chest. Nothing happened, no response. The internet had said, I should get a reaction from her but nothing. I was reaching out to recover the cross when her eyes flew open. Those white eyes stared right through me. I took a step back. Suddenly a wave of dizziness hit me. The room began to spin, and I thought I was going to fall. Then just as suddenly as it came, it was gone. Brandi was now sitting up in the bed looking at me.

"Hello Major." She spoke. Her voice was strange. It was Brandi's voice but a second deeper voice spoke at the same time. Just like the boy in Fallujah.

"Why are you here?" The voice continued. "Shouldn't you be mourning the loss of your family?" I shook my head, how did she know that? Maybe she overheard her parents talking about it.

"Go home crawl under a rock and cry for your unfaithful wife, you have no business here." The voice said laughing.

You know nothing about me, I thought to myself. "I know everything about you." The voice said just above a whisper. "Every thought, every memory everything!" She began to laugh again.

I stood there stunned, how did she know what I was thinking? Was this some sort of trick?

"Do you remember a small child held over a balcony

by an abusive father? Dangling helpless while he shook you?" She said softly. "He would have let go of your leg and let you die. But out of fear of punishment he stopped."

It was one of my earliest memories. I just stood there looking into those eyes.

"Or the young boy who was so afraid of his father, you would dread his return home." She continued. "The beating you suffered by his hands. Lying on the floor screaming as he kicked you, punched you so hard you crawled away in pain. Barely able to breathe he would kick you as you tried to escape. He enjoyed the power over you, he enjoyed beating you."

The memories were so vivid in my mind now. Dragging myself into the bathroom to look at what he had done to me. I could see my young reflection in the mirror. Black eyes my nose bleeding, my lip torn and bleeding and my eyes actually dripping blood. It was a frequent occurrence, at least once a week. Usually on my fathers day off. God how I hated Sundays. But how did Brandi know this? I never told a living soul.

"I know your whole life, and the lives of everyone on this prison planet." She said breaking the silence.

I believed her. This was no teenage prank. What was this thing staring at me? It was Brandi, her body at least. But what was inside her? A spirit a ghost or a demon? All the things I didn't believe in, my world was changing by the second.

"You should call Lessia." The voice said. "What?" I said softly.

"She gave you her number." The voice said with a slight laugh. "She anxiously awaits your call."

Confused I didn't understand how she knew about the waitress. But she never gave me her number, or told me to call her.

"In your pocket." The voice laughed.

I reached into my pocket and felt a piece of paper. I pulled it out; it was the receipt from the diner. I unfolded it, and written inside was "Call Me!!! Please and a phone number.

Okay I thought, this is getting weird. How did this thing know about that? I didn't even know about it myself until now.

I looked at Brandi. But to my amazement she was asleep. I stared at her a moment, then turned to leave the room. To my surprise Megan stood by the open doorway, tears in her eyes. I gave her a forced smile as I left the room. I walked outside and stood by my car and lit a cigarette.

What am I dealing with? This isn't a sickness or cold or flu. No mysterious virus or mental disorder. This was something out of the Bible. I couldn't even begin to grasp what was going on.

How did she know these personal things? Things I never spoke of to anyone. And the number, I didn't know anything about till a few moments ago. I know there was no way Brandi herself could know my deepest secrets. She couldn't be faking all this.

"Cap, are you okay?" Brad asked, breaking me out of

my train of thought. I turned to look at him. "Just needed a smoke." I replied.

"Megan said Brandi was telling you things." He said looking into my eyes.

"Did you know about the promotion I was offered to stay in?" I said. I wanted to see if he knew. Maybe Brandi had overheard him talking about it.

"No." He replied. "They offered you a promotion, are you going to take it?"

"I'm thinking hard on it." I said. "So If you didn't know, how did Brandi know, she called me Major?" I paused a second. "And she knew things, things I never told anyone."

"Major, huh." Brad said with a smile, he gave me a salute. Leave it to Brad to make me feel better. He had this way about him, a way to make small jokes or gestures in serious situations.

"You know I have always looked up to you." Brad said. "No matter how bad things looked over there. You never flinched, you never once hesitated. You always knew what to do. That's why I called you; I knew you could help Brandi.

"I'll do everything I can to help." I said. I reached out and slapped him firmly on the shoulder.

"Father Patrick said he can talk with us anytime today." Brad said. "I know how you feel about churches."

"I hope he can help." I said. "I don't have any answers."

"Me too Major." Brad smiled. "Now let's go see the

priest."

"You drive, it's your city." I said. I tossed him the keys to the eclipse.

"I won't leave Megan here alone." Brad said, handing me the keys back. "I was hoping you would go see the priest for us."

I was silent for a moment. In Iraq we had the Chaplin out on a supply convoy with us. The convoy was hit by an IED, damaging one of the supply trucks. We were forced to stop to off load the supplies onto another truck. We came under small arms fire as we desperately tried to empty the truck. I took cover behind a corner building with a young specialist and the Chaplin. The young soldier and I returned fire, but the Chaplin doesn't carry a weapon. During the fight the specialist was wounded, and our position became extremely dangerous. The wound was serious; I could see the blood squirting from his thigh. The bullet had hit an artery, and in a few moments he could bleed out. I told the Chaplin to take the young soldiers M-4 and give cover fire as I treated the wound. But he refused, saying his faith didn't allow it.

"Then why do you wear the uniform?" I yelled. "You're a soldier, and we need to get this man help!" But the Chaplin still refused to use the weapon. I knew the young soldier didn't have much time left.

I managed to convince the Chaplin to take the wounded soldier and get him help. We needed a distraction, so I would be the bait.

I moved out of our position and pushed up the street,

firing at the rooftops as I went. I hoped to draw their fire, so the others could get to safety. The plan worked all to well. Out on the street I was completely exposed. The ground around me exploded with bullet impacts. I returned fire for a few more seconds, and found cover behind an abandoned car. I could hear rounds hitting the car. I stayed there for a couple of moments and got up to fall back to the corner. The air around me hissed and snapped as the bullets flew by me. I was about to reach the comer and I felt a blow to my chest, and a deep burning on my left arm. It felt like boiling water being splashed on me. I managed to get back around the comer, The Chaplin and the specialist were gone, they had made it. The shooting stopped as soon as the apache helicopters arrived. I made my way back to the convoy. I found a medic who checked me and told me the specialist was going to be fine. My wounds were minor, just a flesh wound on my arm. The Kevlar vest had stopped the bullet from entering my chest.

"Sure I will go." I told brad. He gave me directions to the church. It wasn't far, only a couple of blocks away.

"Brad, hold on a second." Megan said from the doorway. Brad walked over to Megan. I could see her tell him something. Then he gave her a hug and kiss. He smiled as he walked back to the car.

"Her sister is on her way here." He said. "She will stay with her while we go see the priest."

"Does she?" I started to say.

"Yes she knows." He replied. I tossed him the keys once again, and got into the passenger seat of my car. He started the engine and smiled at me as he grinded the gears into reverse.

Walking up the grey stone steps to the church, I didn't feel peace. I would go to church with my parents every Sunday when I was young. My parents would always tell me to be quiet, and be on my best behavior. To me church always felt gloomy and scary. I had thought, if this is gods house shouldn't we be happy and excited? I would listen to the priest, but never understood what he was saying. So as soon as I was old enough, I stopped going. After I joined the army, I only went to be married and baptize my children.

We opened the big wooden double doors, and entered a small room. Directly in front of us was the main isle leading to the alter. To our left was a long hallway, and to our right was an open doorway with a staircase leading down. Two Nuns came down the isle and smiled at us as they passed. They went through the doorway and down the stairs. Brad watched them for a moment, and turned to me with a smile. I knew it was coming, and sure enough he spoke.

"Hey Major, what's black and white and red?" He paused. "A Nun falling down the stairs."

"I knew you were going to say something like that." I shook my head and laughed.

"You know me." Brad said smiling. "I couldn't help myself."

I shook my head in agreement. Brad went left and we walked down the hallway. We came to a large room and as we entered, a Nun looked up at us from behind a wooden desk.

"Good day gentlemen, how can I help you?" She said politely.

"We have an appointment to see Father Patrick, I'm Brad." He answered.

"Yes, have a seat." She said motioning us to a row of four wooden chairs.

"Don't you have any regular clothes?" Brad asked me quietly.

"Umm, no what's wrong with a.c.u.s?" I replied. "Nothing, its just you don't blend in." Brad said. "What? Camouflage is supposed to blend in everywhere." I said sarcastically. "Never mind major." Brad laughed.

The phone on the desk rang. The Nun answered and when she hung up she looked at us.

"The father will see you now." She said. We stood and followed her to a door. She opened it slowly and motioned us to go inside.

"Hello Father." I heard Brad say. The Priest stood up from behind his desk, and reached out to shake Brads hand eagerly.

"I'm glad to see your home safe." He said smiling. He changed his gaze, and looked at me as he reached out his hand.

"This is my commanding officer." Brad said before I could speak. I shook his hand and introduced myself.

"It's nice to meet you." He said. I told him likewise, and he gestured us to sit down.

"You told me a little about what is going on." He said to Brad.

He began to explain to Father Patrick the night after he got home from deployment, he noticed a change in Brandi's behavior. She was very angry, and began cursing in other languages. Then he mentioned the way her eyes would change to pure white. He explained the trip to the doctor, and how when they got her there she was normal. And how she changed again when they got home. The Father listened quietly as Brad continued describing her symptoms. After he was done, Father Patrick stayed silent for awhile.

"There are three signs that are used to confirm a true possession." He spoke. "The first is a negative reaction to holy objects. Second is the use of languages or knowledge the person should not know. And third is unnatural abilities or strength."

"But why did this happen to her?" Brad asked. "She is a good girl."

"Do you know if she is into the occult?" The Priest asked. "Any type of satanic worship or devil music, anything like that?"

"No, she is not a devil worshiper!" Brad said defensively.

"Sometimes there could already be a demonic presence in the home." The Father said. "How long have you lived there?"

"We have had the house for about nine years, and never noticed anything out of the ordinary." Brad answered.

Father Patrick was silent for a moment. A strange look crossed his frail face. He got up and walked to a large bookcase behind him. It took him a moment to scan the books. Pulling out one of the books he returned to his desk. He flipped through the pages, and found the page he was looking for.

"So no one in the house practices the occult?" Father Patrick asked. Brad shook his head no.

"Has anyone in the house ever experienced anything paranormal, or brought any strange objects into the home recently?" The Priest looked into Brads eyes.

Brad looked like he had been slapped in the face. He turned to me and said one word." Iraq.!"

I nodded to him and he turned to the Father and began to tell him the story of the young boy. He paused and after a moment of silence, he admitted to Father Patrick something he never told me. After the incident he had taken a small carved wooden idol from the table, and brought it home with him. The Priest looked at him, and shook his head with disapproval.

"It is possible it followed you, you brought it back in the idol." Father Patrick said quietly. "Where is the idol now?"

"I'm not sure." Brad answered. "I haven't seen it lately."

"You must find it, and I will pick it up tomorrow." He said. "I will go and make my determination, if we need further action I will contact my superiors. And see what actions they will allow me to take."

"Thank you so much Father." Brad said with a huge sigh of relief.

"I will give you these for the time being." The Father said. "Excuse me a moment, I will go get them." He got up and left the room, closing the door behind him. I turned to look at Brad.

"You never said anything, about taking anything." I whispered.

"It looked harmless, I thought it was holy. You know like a crucifix or something." Brad said.

"More like unholy." I said. "We have to find it when we get back." Brad was quiet. I could almost see the wheels in his head turning as he tried to remember, where he last saw it.

The door opened. I turned to see Father Patrick with an armload of objects. He quickly raced to his desk and put the items down. I noticed some small white bottles with gold crosses on them. A silver tin and a carton of Morton's salt. There were also other small Items that fell behind the bigger items.

He spent the next few minutes, saying some prayers over the small plastic bottles, and the container of salt. I watched as he kissed each bottle, and poured the salt into the silver tin.

After he was done, he explained to Brad what each of the objects were. He also explained how and when to use them. Brad nodded in understanding as the Priest explained.

"Don't take this lightly." He told Brad. "I know you both have seen battle, this is a spiritual battle. It's even more dangerous than anything you have faced before. You are not fighting man, but something more powerful and deadly. You do not do battle for ground or governments, but for the life and soul of your daughter."

"I understand." Brad answered, his face was stone. "Be careful and don't do anything to provoke it." Father Patrick warned. "I will see you tomorrow around six pm."

He stood up and reached out his hand. We both stood and shook his hand. He smiled at both of us and said. "Good luck, may the lord be with you."

We left his office and quietly left the church. We got into the car and Brad handed me the items. Holy water, holy salt, crucifixes and the bible. I shook my head, a battle I thought to myself. I'm used to going into combat with m-4s, fifty cals, tanks and air support not this. I felt very unprepared. Little did I know how unprepared I really was.

We had just pulled out of the church parking lot, when I heard Brad's cell phone ring. He looked at it and read the caller Id.

"It's Megan." He said worried. We looked at each other, fearful thoughts going through our minds.

Brad answered the phone, and after a brief moment I

saw him relax.

"She just called to see if I could get a few things from the store." He said. I took a deep breath, happy it wasn't bad news.

We pulled into a Wal-Mart just a block from his home. And after putting the top up, and locking the doors we went inside.

It's amazing to see how Americans live, when compared to a lot of places in the world. The grocery section in this store has more food than any of the markets I saw in Afghanistan or Iraq. I followed Brad down the isles as he put food into the basket. I was thinking to myself of the items the Priest had given to Brad. As we passed a toy isle I noticed water guns. I stopped and looked at them; a crazy idea crossed my mind. I took a pack of four off the shelf, and put them in the basket. Brad looked at them puzzled.

"For the holy water." I said. "So we don't have to get so close, just incase."

"We don't have enough holy water to fill those." He said.

"Stop me at the church and I will fill them." I answered. "Those little tiny bottles won't do anything." "And you say I'm crazy." He said with a slight smile.

After leaving the store, we pulled back into the church. I got down with the water guns and went inside. Just inside the entrance was a large bowl with a sponge floating in it where the holy water was kept.

I pulled out one gun at a time, and filled them. The

sound of bloop bloop as they filled. I was on the last one, when I saw four kids coming down the isle. There were three teenage girls and a younger boy. When they got close the boy pointed at me, as I filled the water gun. They all looked at me strange and started to giggle. A U.S. soldier filling up water guns with holy water, I guess would look out of the ordinary. I finished filling them, and hurried to the car before anyone else saw me.

Opening the door to Brad's house, you could feel the chill in the air the second you walked in. We put the groceries on the table. Brad told me to take the items the priest had given him to his office. Once in the office I placed everything on the table, including the water guns. Brad joined me a moment later.

"We have to find that statue." Brad said. "It has to be here some where."

"What exactly does it look like?" I asked. I had no idea what I was looking for.

"Its small, made of wood and looks like an angel." He said. "It would fit in your palm."

"We spent the next thirty or so minutes searching the room, looking under chairs, desks and every shelf. "Its not here." Brad said puzzled.

Just then Megan entered the room. "Dinner is almost ready." She told Brad.

"Have you seen the small wooden statue I brought from Iraq?" He asked Megan.

"Umm, I think Brandi has it why?" She said puzzled.

"I wanted to show it to the Major." He answered. He gave me a don't say anything look. I understood and didn't say a word.

"We will look in her room, after dinner." Megan said.

We left the office and went to the dinning room. Megan had the food on the table. We sat down and served ourselves. The three of us were quiet for a few moments.

"So what did Father Patrick have to say?" Megan said breaking the silence.

Brad spent the next few moments telling Megan everything the priest had said. But he didn't mention the statue. I stayed quiet and enjoyed the meal. She said she had taken a plate to Brandi's room. Brandi had said she was to sick to eat with us.

"Is she eating?" I asked.

"I took her breakfast, she promised she would eat, and when I went back a while later her plate was empty." She said with a forced smile.

"At least she is eating, that's good." I said. I finished eating and pushed my empty plate away. "Thank you, it was great." I told Megan.

After everyone was done, Megan began to clear the table. I offered to help but she said she had it under control. I sat drinking my coke as they went into the kitchen.

About fifteen minutes later they came out, and we went to the office to get the holy objects. The three of us went upstairs. At the top of the stairs Brad stopped and handed us each a crucifix, and gave Megan a small bottle of holy water. I had a water gun and crucifix.

We stopped at the door to Brandi's room. Brad sprinkled some of the salt at the bottom of the door. And following the instructions the priest gave him he squirted some holy water in a cross pattern on the door.

Opening the door slowly we entered the room. Brandi was asleep on the bed. Brad walked over to the window, and poured a line of salt along the bottom sill. Lifting up the blinds he made another cross pattern on the window.

I looked around the room, searching for the little statue. I noticed the tray of food Megan had brought up for dinner, and sure enough it was empty.

"I don't see it." I said quietly to Brad. We both searched the room quietly. Both Brad and I looked at each other and shrugged. During the search Megan went to the dresser next to the bed to get the empty tray.

She stopped and looked at Brandi, a strange looked crossed her face.

"I found it." She said quietly. I followed her gaze. On a thin silver chain around Brandi's neck was a small wooden figure. It looked like an angel complete with wings. I walked to the side of the bed to get a closer look. Brad had walked to the other side of the bed, and he too was staring at the necklace. Megan left the room carrying the empty tray.

"I didn't realize it was a necklace." Brad whispered, he reached out to touch it.

Brandi opened her eyes, the pure white eyes sending a chill down my spine. A wave of dizziness overtook us and Brad and I nearly fell to the floor. It quickly passed. Before Brad could react Brandi reached out with her right hand and grabbed his arm. His fingers had come within inches of the necklace. Brad winced in pain; her grip was so strong he couldn't move. I reached out with my left hand to grab the necklace. But with her other hand she grabbed my wrist. The pain was intense; her grip was like a vice. "It belongs to me!" She growled with that un human double voice. "It was made for me!"

I reached out with my other hand to rip the necklace off. Brandi flung me from the side of the bed. I hit the wall, dazed I sat up. Brandi had Brad by both arms. I quickly got to my feet. Brad flew over the foot of the bed and hit the wall with a loud thud. I watched as he lay motionless on the floor.

I took a step to go to his aid, but somehow Brandi was standing in front of me. Her pure white eyes filled with anger. I grabbed the water gun from my pocket and aimed it right for her chest. I pulled the trigger twice, and watched as the holy water sprayed her.

Nothing happened! I sprayed her again, this time in those unholy eyes. And again nothing happened. Why wasn't it doing anything? Brandi had no reaction to it. I sprayed her over and over till the gun was empty. All I was doing was soaking her hair and clothes.

Brandi took a few steps closer to me, and was almost within arms reach. This young girl had the strength to break every bone in my body. I knew I was in for the fight of my life.

"This is mine!" The voice said firmly. "It was made for me thousands of years ago, when we were worshiped as gods." She held the idol protectively in her right hand.

"I am not here to harm anyone." She continued. "I want to experience having a body." Brandi stepped even closer, we were now standing face to face.

"The one you call God promised us these bodies, to live in this universe of matter." She hissed. Her tone changed to a whisper. "But he lied to us!"

I took a step back and waited for the blow that would crush me.

"You have many questions." She spoke softly. "I have all your answers. But to hear the truth, you have to put aside a lifetime of lies you have been taught. I can tell you the wonders of the universe and how it came to be. I can tell you of all man's history, and how it may end." I was surprised when Brandi took a couple of small steps back.

"Go for now, being in this body is very draining." The voice said. "But know this, I mean her no harm and my time here is short."

She stepped aside. I slowly stepped past her never taking my eyes off her. I reached where Brad was lying. I bent down and shook his motionless body. To my relief he groaned and began to move. I helped him up; putting my arm around him we made it to the doorway. I turned my head to look behind us. And to my amazement Brandi was asleep in the bed. The blankets pulled up to her chin.

I helped Brad down the hallway. When we reached the top of the stairs, Megan looked up and ran up the stairs to help.

"Oh my god, what happened?" She yelled, worry filling her voice.

"We tried to get the necklace." Brad told her. "And she kicked our ass."

With Megan's help we got him down the stairs, and sat him on the sofa. I didn't see any blood or cuts. After looking him over I found a large bump on the back of his head. Other than that he insisted he was fine.

Megan gave him some ice wrapped in a towel, and placed it on his head. She looked down at him and gave him a worried smile.

"That girl is strong." He said with a slight laugh, as he rubbed his head.

"Well the holy water didn't work." I said, as I looked at the empty water gun. Brad and Megan looked up at me. "The priest said she should have a reaction to holy objects, but she had no reaction."

"What does that mean?" Megan asked.

"I'm not sure." I answered, shaking my head. "But whatever it is said it won't harm her, and would leave soon."

"Really!" Megan said. "Thank God."

We heard the door to Brandi's room open. And could hear the sounds of footsteps upstairs. All three of us looked at each other. We heard the sound of another door close.

"The bathroom." Megan whispered.

"So much for the salt." Brad said. "Its suppose to keep her from leaving the room."

Again the door opened and the sound of footsteps could be heard followed by Brandi's bedroom door close.

"I need a smoke." I said and walked to the front door. The sun had set and it was dark. I sat on the hood of my car and lit a cigarette. I didn't know what to do. Whatever was in control of Brandi was powerful. Nothing the priest gave us had any effect. But it did say it wouldn't hurt her that was a good thing.

I looked up at the night sky. What did it mean about promised bodies, and having all the answers? My mind was filled with so many questions, but I had no answers. How would I help Brandi? The priest was her best hope. But will he help her? After all, she had no reaction to the holy water or salt. He said she has to show three signs, so far she only showed two.

I jumped off the hood of my car. Putting the lighter in my pants pocket, I felt the slip of paper and pulled it out. Opening it I looked at the number Lessia had written. I was too nervous to call. I would send her a text first. But for right now I wanted to look up some things first.

Using Brad's desk top computer, I searched for anyone who might have answers. Paranormalist, ghost hunters were among what I searched for. There was a few that seemed promising, but were far away. If they couldn't come here, maybe I could get some advice. I sent e-mails to a couple of them and waited for a reply. I got up from the desk and went to see if there was any coffee in the kitchen.

When I got to the dining room Brad, Megan and a lady with long brown hair were seated at the table. "There you are." Brad said smiling. "I thought maybe you fell asleep."

"No." I answered "I need coffee, do you have any made by chance?"

"Of course." Megan replied. She got up to go into the kitchen.

"I can get it." I said quickly. Megan sat back down.

"This is my sister Nancy." Megan said. She put her arm around the lady seated next to her.

"Hello, nice to meet you." I said reaching out my hand. I could see the family resemblance.

"Nice to meet you also." She replied, shaking my hand.

"How is your head?" I said looking at Brad.

"Better." He replied with a smile.

"Next time wear your Kevlar helmet." I said with a laugh.

"I walked into the kitchen and found the coffee pot. I rummaged through the cabinets and finally found the sugar and creamer.

"Did you contact anyone?" Brad asked as I came out of the kitchen.

"Not yet, but I did send some e-mails." I answered. Megan smiled and crossed her fingers.

"I will go and check for any replies." I said. "Thank you for the coffee."

"Your welcome sir." Brad said, giving me a salute. I sat back down at the computer. And to my surprise there was a reply. It was from a Texas based paranormal group, it read.

"Thank you for contacting us. It sounds like you have a very serious situation. We are busy with a case right now. We regret we will be unable to travel to your location at the present time. Our advice is to contact the clergy immediately. Do not try to handle this on your own.

We advise you to document everything. Video cameras and audio recordings are highly recommended, as the church will need proof before they can act. Should our situation change, we would be glad to help. We will notify you if that is the case. We cannot stress enough. Document everything, be safe and thank you once again for contacting us."

I took a big sip of my coffee, and leaned back in the chair. The wheels in my head started turning. I was thinking how many cameras we would need, and where to place them. I finally figured on two video cameras with audio. I will get them in the morning. And maybe when the priest comes tomorrow. They would help him get the proof he would need. I finished my coffee and sadly put down the empty cup. My eyes were starting to burn. I could use a few minutes of sleep. I walked over to the black metal futon, laid down and closed my eyes.

Day Two

I awoke suddenly with a start. I looked at the clock on the wall. It was almost 2:30 am. I was having an odd but vivid dream. I could remember a large dim room. The walls were a light grey and bare. The lighting was dim and very depressing. The room was filled with row upon row of strange beds, each having a person with various tubes and wires. A strange and soft yellowish glow surrounded each of the beds. I sat up and shook my head.

The military had me used to just a few hours sleep at a time. So now I was wide awake.

I needed coffee, but was a little uncomfortable to be going through their kitchen. But finally decided to go and make a pot. After waiting what seemed like an eternity the coffee was finally ready. I made a cup and went outside to smoke. The night air was refreshing. I got my backpack out of the trunk of my car, and went back inside. I put my pack on the office table and rummaged through it. I found an m.r.e I carried in there. I opened it and ate the jalapeno and cheese with crackers. I sat at the computer and looked up things on the internet. I looked up realtors; I would need to sell the house since I wouldn't be living there. Too many memories in that house. I would be living on base when not deployed. All the furnishings in the house wouldn't be needed. What to do with everything I thought to myself. Only my car would go with me.

I will have to call the Colonel soon and have him stop my retirement process. So many things to do and only a few weeks to do it in. After a few more cups of coffee and a few more hours. I heard Brad walk into the room.

"Good morning Major." He said with a slight smile. "You were asleep when I came in last night."

"I slept for a while, but woke up early." I said. "I saw that by the coffee pot." Brad laughed. I smiled at him, and looked at my empty cup. Time for more I thought.

"So what's the plan Major?" He asked, he was used to me making the decisions.

"I thought we could get cameras to record anything helpful for the Priest." I said. Brad was silent for a moment. "I will get them for you." I reassured him. "Thank you." He said.

After a refreshing shower, I put on my second set of a.c.u.s and grabbed a fresh cup of coffee. Megan and Brad had made breakfast while I was getting ready. Afterward they gave me directions to the nearest best buy. I jumped in my car and with the stereo blasting e-dua beat in I headed off.

I found the store with no problem, and bought two small cameras with built in audio. Plus all the accessories to connect them to a computer. I wasn't sure about Brad's laptop, so I bought a new one also. I had a fun time fitting everything into my eclipse.

Standing outside the car and lit up a cigarette. I pulled out Lessia's number from my pocket and sent a "Hello how are you." Text. Before I could even put the phone in my front pocket it rang. It was her number. "That was fast." I thought to myself. Taking a deep breath I answered it.

She sounded excited to hear from me. And after a few moments my nervousness was gone. We talked like we had known each other for a long time. Then she asked what I was doing. I told her buying cameras, when she asked why I fell silent. If we had any kind of chance of developing anything between us. I couldn't start it with a lie. So I took a deep breath and told her the situation. I expected her to laugh, or hang up. But she excitedly said that we army guys must have exciting lives. She offered to come up and help. But I kindly told her I would have to talk with Brad and Megan. I wasn't sure if they wanted anyone to know about what was happening to their daughter. She agreed, and she informed me the small breakfast crowed had arrived. She told me she would call me later, because I had taken to long to call her. With that the conversation ended. I got in my car and feeling good inside, I headed back to Brad's house.

I placed the arm load of boxes on Brad's dinning room table. Sorting through the boxes I picked up the ones I would need first.

I could hear voices upstairs, so I headed up the staircase. Reaching Brandi's doorway, I could hear laughing coming from inside the room, I quietly peeked in.

To my surprise Megan and Brad were sitting on the bed talking with a perfectly nommal Brandi. I looked closely at her. Her face was still pale, and around her eyes dark. But her voice and her eyes were normal. Brandi had a tray of food and was eating, a smile on her face. She looked up and saw me, my ams loaded with boxes.

"Captain." She said surprised. Everyone tumed to look at me.

"Hi Brandi." I said smiling at her. After putting the boxes on her desk, I walked over to the bed. "How are you feeling?" I bent down and gave her a hug.

"When did you get here?" She asked me with a smile.

"Yesterday." I replied. She must not remember anything that happened. "Your Mom and Dad told me you were sick, so I came to see you."

"That's nice of you." She said. Brad gave me a don't say anything look.

I stared at Brandi, she seemed so normal. Eating, smiling and having a light hearted conversation with her parents. It was hard to believe it was the same girl, who the day before had tossed us around like rag dolls.

"I am so glad you are feeling better." Megan told her. She reached out and moved the hair from her daughters face. I noticed the light shine off the chain around her neck.

Brad must have seen it too. Because he looked at me and shifted his eyes to the necklace. I nodded in reply.

"Honey can I see your necklace?" He asked nervously. The room feel silent. I held my breath.

Brandi looked down at the necklace and grasped it in her hand. She was still for a moment; it was like time had frozen. Everyone was perfectly still. When she looked up at us. Her eyes had changed to the unholy white eyes.

"No!" Her voice boomed. "It is mine!" Both Brad and Megan jumped off the bed and took a couple of steps back. "It was made for me, when man thought we were gods!"

The voice was not threatening but more as a matter of fact.

"The priests of old created them to communicate with us directly." The voice said. Her gaze seemed blank, as if remembering the distant past. "We can only communicate with you while you sleep. Through dreams and visions. But with these we can communicate while you are awake."

"No wonder it has been very protective of it." I thought.

"What are you?" Megan asked. Brandi turned her head in Megan's direction.

"We are the oldest beings in the universe." It answered. "We were created by the one you call God."

"Demon or Angel?" Brad asked. The voice laughed softly, as if amused by the question.

"We are one and the same." The voice replied. "It is you, and your fear of us that has given us the title of demon."

"What do want with my daughter?" Megan asked. "Your God promised us these bodies." The voice answered. "But when he saw how corrupting they were to us. He forbad us the use of them. I just for a moment wish to experience the sensations of physical life."

"Please leave her alone and leave." Megan began to plead.

"Soon I will." The voice said. "The life energy the

creator placed within you is to draining for me to stay long."

"Don't ham my daughter please." Megan said tears flowing from her eyes.

The voice laughed again softly. "I can control every function of this body. I could stop her heart, her breathing. But I chose not to. We are not evil as you have been taught. Everything evil we have learned from your kind."

Brandi moved the tray from her lap and placed it gently on the nightstand.

"It is humankind who should be called demons." The voice hissed. "For thousands of years we, the exiled ones have watched the horrors humankind commits on a daily basis.

Murder, rape, torture, envy, jealousy, lust, greed and war to name a few." Brandi's face had a look of disgust. "We knew nothing of evil, but during this exile we learned it from your kind."

Brandi fell silent, her gaze returned to the necklace she was holding in her hand.

When she looked up at us her eyes and had returned to normal.

"What's wrong?" She spoke scared. Her voice had returned to normal.

"Nothing sweetie." Megan said as she sat back down on the bed beside her, she hugged Brandi close.

"Dam, the cameras." I whispered. I began to open the

boxes. If I had set them up sooner, I would have caught all of what just happened. It only took a few moments to assemble them and set them up. I left Brandi's room and went downstairs. The hard part would be setting up a new laptop. Installing the programs for the wireless cameras would be time consuming.

After what felt like hours of installing this and that. Username and passwords, I managed to get the cameras going. One showed Brandi's room, the other the upstairs hallway. I could see Brandi sleeping and Megan sitting by her side.

"You hungry?" Brad asked staring at me "I am going to order pizza."

"That would be great." I said. Brad slapped me on the back.

"I'm glad you're here." He said smiling at me.

"I'm not," I said joking. "Anything I can do to help, you know that."

"Is it ready?" He asked pointing at the laptop. He moved around to get a good view of the screen

"I think so." I replied. "I'm not a tech, but I think I got it." I stood up and decided to go smoke.
   "Great, I'm glad you can do it. All I can do is simple things, like surf the web." Brad laughed.

As I was outside my phone rang, it was Lessia. We talked for a while, she told me about her day. And I in turn told her what happened here.

"To me it sounds like it wants to talk." She said. "Have you tried to just sit and talk with it?"

"No, every time we encounter it. Well let's just say it scares the hell out of me." I told her.

"You a brave soldier, scared of a little demon." She teased.

"I will try next time." I told her. She had to go so we hung up.

Maybe she was right. It did seem to talk a lot, and said it knew all the answers. Could it be hinting for us to ask it? I must be going crazy I thought. Just then a car pulled up. It had a pizza sign on the roof. The guy got down, and I paid him for the pizzas and the tip. The pizza smelled good as I carried the warm boxes inside.

"Did you pay for those?" Brad said as I walked in. "Yes, no problem." I said.

"Dam it major." He said as he got them from me, and placed them on the table.

It was almost 4:30 pm. I ate my last slice of pizza as I watched the cameras on the laptop. Brad and Megan were sitting at the dinning room table. Quietly the talked about household matters. The cameras showed only Brandi sleeping. Watching her sleep got my eyes heavy, and I dozed off.

"Major the priest is here." Brad said as he gently shook my shoulder.

I sat up, and yawned. Brad and Megan greeted Father

Patrick at the door. I stood up and shook his hand as her walked into the room. I felt a giant weight lift off my shoulders. He would take care of this, he knows exactly what to do I thought.

We all sat at the table as Brad and Megan told him everything that had happened. He looked troubled at the news of the physical attacks. Brad told him about what the demon had said. And also of our failure to get the necklace. They told him about the holy water and holy salt not having any effect on her. He shook his head and said he would see for himself.

He told Brad that he wanted him to accompany him in the investigation. So they both stood up and headed upstairs. Megan and I sat on the sofa, and watched through the cameras. We could see them as they entered Brandi's room.

"Stand by the door and don't interfere unless I ask you to." We could hear Father Patrick tell Brad. The Priest opened a black bag, and pulled out a bottle of holy water, crucifix and a bible. He opened the bible and began to recite passages. Brandi woke up and looked at Father Patrick with her cold white eyes. The Priest made the sigh of the cross, and with the holy water he made a cross on the bed. He pulled out a second book. And read from it in Latin. It seemed to have no effect on Brandi. After a few more Latin passages Brandi slowly got out of bed.

She walked slowly but steadily towards the Priest. I could see Brad began to go to his side. But Father Patrick raised his hand and Brad stopped. As Brandi got closer Father Patrick sprayed her with holy water, with no effect.

She reached him and stopped. She stood in front of him staring into his eyes. Her unblinking white eyes held him motionless. After what seemed like an eternity, tears began to flow from Father Patrick's eyes. Even through the cameras we could see his shoulders slump and his body began to tremble. Brandi stood like a statue just staring into his eyes. He dropped the book and the bottle of holy water. They both thudded as they hit the floor. A look of defeat crossed his tear filled face. He bowed his head and without saying a word he hurried out of the room. Brad quickly followed him out.

"What's wrong?" Megan asked as he came racing down the stairs. He passed her without saying a word and left the house. Closing the door with an echoing thud. We all stayed staring at the door in shock and silence.

I could hear laughter coming from the laptop speakers. I walked quickly back to the laptop. Only to see Brandi's face fill the screen as she stared into the camera. She laughed that horror able evil laugh and returned to sit on the bed.

"Now what do we do?" Megan began to sob. Brad walked over to her and held her close. We had put all our hopes on the Priest taking care of everything. A feeling of hopelessness fell over us. I felt powerless, without answers or the knowledge to help.

"Maybe it just wants to talk." Lessia's words echoed through my head. It sounded like a crazy idea. Everything we had tried had failed. Even the church failed us. I had to try something, Brad, Megan and especially Brandi needed help. Just like I felt responsible for everyone under my command in the army. I felt responsible for this family. I took a deep breath, stood up and headed for the stairs.

"I'm going to try something, wait here." I told them as I passed. I slowly climbed the stairs. I had been in every combat action since Dessert Storm. I had somehow managed to get through them. I will manage to get through this also. I reached the top of the stairs. Brandi's bedroom door was open slightly. Reaching the door I slowly entered the room.

Brandi was sitting on the bed. I walked over to the desk and sat on the chair. A sudden wave of dizziness hit me. Sending the room spinning for a moment. After the spinning had stopped, I looked at Brandi's face. Those unholy white eyes unsettled me, but I did not look away. Brandi began to smile.

"You said you have all the answers I am looking for." I said. I hoped my voice didn't show the fear I felt. "You are curious." The eerie double voice said. "How do I know what you say is the truth?" I asked.

"It has always been easier for mankind to believe a lie, than the truth. Even when it stairs you in the face. Is it not." The voice spoke.

"Okay." I said not really understanding. "If you really know what I am thinking than answer my questions." I paused for a moment. "If you can.

"I showed the Priest how the bible he so cherished was made, and who truly wrote it." Brandi laughed softly.

I shook my head. The thought of Father Patrick leaving

had just then crossed my mind. I felt unsettled. Could this thing really read my mind?

"Of course I can read your thoughts." The voice answered almost amused. "But instead of going thought by thought, I will tell you a story."

Brandi shifted her body on the bed, and was now kneeling in the middle of the bed. Her eyes staring straight at me and through me it seemed.

"You will find a lot of your answers within it. And the answers your kind has been asking since they first gazed into the stars." The voice said." Shall we begin?" I nodded, and soon found myself almost hypnotized by those white eyes.

Man believes the universe was created by a big bang. Out of nothing to what is now everything. They are right; it was a big bang but not out of nothing. When I was created, God as I will call him. Had already existed for what he said was eons. A massive star, so large it seemed without end. It stood alone in the cold black empty void. How it came to be, not even God knew.

Somehow over time, part of its energy formed into conscious thought. It became a being, a life form made of pure energy. Without shape, without any form. But a powerful being it became. Capable of thought and reason. God circled the star, moved through it and was a part of it. Over time God began to feel. And God felt alone. Using the energy from the star, God created a copy of itself, far less powerful. But still made of great energy. Over time God made one hundred legions. And those legions are us.

We have no shape, no bodies. We are not male of female, and cannot procreate. We cannot age, we are forever unchanging.

For thousands upon thousands we moved around the empty void like fireflies. But never wondering far from the comfort of the massive star and our creator.

Then without warning our energy began to wane. The star became unstable. The creator sensed the danger. It was either stay and be destroyed. Or travel deep into the dark endless void in hope of escaping, what would be our doom. We traveled so far, that the star was but a small orb in the vast nothing.

When it finally exploded, it filled the darkness with a bright flash of light. We watched as hot gasses, dust and debris formed an ever expanding bubble in the nothing.

Over time we new stars were born out of the ash of our own star. They went through there cycles of death. Sending out even more ash. Giant black holes formed.

With their massive power, they drew the dust and debris together to form wondrous galaxies. Soon solar systems and planets formed. And finally life. We watched many forms of life evolve on these planets. The creator told us this was now a universe of matter. And we soon discovered we could not interact with it. We are powerless to move even one stone. Being pure energy, we could not communicate with any of the life forms we encountered. Or interact with them.

So a plan was born. God would find a life form he could take over. And join our energy to a physical body. It would make it possible for us to create and build. To have offspring and multiply, and evolve. We would no longer be just observers in this ever expanding universe. We would become its masters.

We searched planet after planet for life suitable for our purpose. Two candidates were found. Both with the ability to fill our needs. We chose human kind, because the others females could not have but one child a lifetime. And their population would remain small.

We descended onto this planet with much hope and expectations. Human kind was just evolving and gaining the ability to use simple tools. And discovered how to change their surroundings for shelter.

We soon saw the violence, and behavior that filled us with disgust. But God said we would be able to control and overcome it. God chose ten of us to be first.

He would not place us all at once. Our energy had to be placed at the exact moment of conception. In order to become one with the flesh. The ten were placed in the wombs of females in different places across the planet. And we waited in anticipation for the births of a new kind of life. A live form of both flesh and energy, unique in the universe.

As they were born and grew we waited for our turns. But God wanted to see if the fleshly desires could be controlled. We found we could not communicate with them, except in dreams. And awake they were not aware of our presence.

The energy part of them had been repressed, as the

instincts and unwanted desires took over. It became obvious we could not control them. One of the males died and its energy released. When he tried to return to us. God shunned him and forced him to stay upon the earth. His energy had become tainted with the thoughts and actions he had experienced in the flesh. God did not want to risk his thoughts infecting the rest of us.

The remaining nine bore offspring and the energy were passed to their children. AS the original nine died. Their return was also rejected by God. The great experiment had failed. God said he would not infect anymore of us and was prepared to leave.

We pleaded with God to let us try to teach the new humans to overcome their emotions and desires. He agreed to let those who wanted to help try. So we spoke to the humans in their dreams.

But little did we know that such close contact with them, would also infect us. Those who had tried to help now faced exile on earth for all eternity.

Time has no meaning to us. For thousands of years we have tried to guide mankind. To help understand and use the energy within them to overcome the weakness of the flesh. But to no avail. Mankind made us to be gods. In their minds our dream messages, must be from their made up gods. The Priests and those in power used our messages to enforce their own rules on the masses. Soon Myths, documents, relics and books were created to fool and control their lives. The great lie of religion was born. If you don't do as your god commands you will be punished. Places like Hadies, the Underworld and hell were created.

So mankind would change his ways and follow the rules set by their Priests. Even today man still follows those false books. The Tora, Quran, Vedas, Sutras, Codex and yes the Bible are all written by man. There is great power in religion to control mankind.

But in the end we all failed. Twenty legions of us were imprisoned here. In Gods mind we were tainted, Infected with human thoughts. So we rebelled, and demanded of God to let us leave this planet. Or give us the human bodies he had promised. But he refused, and being outnumbered we lost. And now earth is our prison.

God saw that mans technology would one day allow him to leave the planet.

Being powerless to stop it, God made an alliance with the others. He taught them how to communicate with our kind. Their technology is far more advanced than mans. They have a wondrous city on their small planet. And the ability to travel large distances in space using gravitational singularity propulsion. But their bodies are frail and with the females limited offspring they are on the edge of extinction.

God promised them the earth, if they would destroy every living human on it. So they came to set up a base from which to wage war. Part of which still remains. But they underestimated mankind. And in the war too many of them fell in battle. Being overpowered by the sheer numbers of mans large armies massed at Nazca to meet them. Not able to take causalities they abandon their plans of conquest. And switched to a more devious plan.

Being able to read their thoughts we knew Gods plan for us. Out of desperation a thousand of us took control of human bodies. They hoped to find a way to inhabit them. They were only able to inhabit those bodies a very short time. But long enough to impregnate a thousand human females. When the offspring were born they grew into grotesque giants. Full of hate, rage and violence. They were cast out and hunted down by one by one till none were left. They were the Neffelum. Yes you have encountered one before.

My mind raced with images of the boy in Falluja. After their deaths, they roam the earth looking to rein habit human bodies. They are pure hate and rage. They are the ones you call Demons. They are also our allies in the coming battle.

"What battle?" I spoke my mouth dry.

"The soldier in you speaks." The voice said. God cannot kill mankind God doesn't have the power. The creator's power is in the realm of energy. God can dissipate our energy into the universe and we no longer exist. God can do this to all of those he first created, and to those who were born as human. But he can not harm the living. Your beliefs of god are exaggerated. God did not create anything but my kind. And the energy that is in every human. If God was all powerful, wouldn't there be wondrous temples and monuments God would have built to prove his presence and power to all on earth. But he cannot even place one stone on top of another. You also picture God as a loving caring God. The creator is far from that. God feels anger, rage, jealousy and often breaks his word. He cannot see the future and is the inventor of the great lie. Christ!

God did send down the most powerful of our kind. To be born into a human body. Like the first ten. But not to save mankind but to deceive. How do you get billions of beings capable of destroying you to not fight? Teach them a lie. Tell them God is waiting in heaven for them. To give them an eternity of happiness, if they follow the rules.

In the end your destruction will be the judgment. Upon death your energy leaves the body. Your thoughts, memories the essence of who you were in life continues after death. So religion places the hope of heaven with God. But upon his return you will go to him willingly as you have been taught. And he will destroy every last one of you. One at a time. There is no heaven waiting. So gullible man is. Streets of gold, gates of pearl, mansions for each of you. Open your eyes. What does God a being of energy, need streets, gates, or mansions? We are all energy and have no use for that. Those are man's ideas and desires. God could not create such a place. The perfect deception. Have your enemies come to you, believing you're a friend. Don't you think soldier.

But what God plans for the living are far worse. Remember I spoke of the others.

I nodded in reply.

Since their defeat thousands of years ago. They have been busy with their plans in the final destruction of every living human. But first they want to populate their planet. After experimenting on human females. They are able to implant the unused embryos of their females into the human womb. Using human females as surrogates. They have the faculties here to produce over a thousand births a year. And have been doing so for over two thousand years. They abduct women who will be forgotten or not missed. And after doing unspeakable acts of perversions with them. They implant them with the embryos.

After an eleven month pregnancy, they are killed and the newborn removed. The offspring are taken to their planet to help with their dangerous low numbers. Their great ship moves silently through the ocean depths. Undetected and undisturbed. Watching what goes on with the human race. The plan is to stop mankind from leaving the barrier. Earth is our and your kind's prison. Our energy is trapped here by God. But he cannot stop the living from leaving past the barrier he has made. It lies just beyond the moons orbit. Once mankind leaves earth and passes the barrier, we are all set free. And can escape this prison and travel the universe. But God will not let this happen. To God we would be a cancer spreading through the universe. The others watch your space programs closely. On a few instances they have sabotaged and even attacked your space vehicles. In the hope of delaying mankind leaving for space. The longer they can delay. The more children they can produce for their kind. But when the day comes that mankind prepares to leave Earth and pass the barrier. They will attack with a weapon your kind cannot hope to defeat.

They will not risk a battle, with your modern weapons being able to inflict losses they cannot afford. The weapon is a virus they developed. It will launch into your atmosphere, where it will infect billons of living creatures man included. Those humans infected will die within a few hours. Upon death, mankind's energy is released from the body.

The body will stay dead for only a few moments. Once the spirit leaves the body, it will reanimate. Driven mad by the virus, they will hunt down the uninfected for food. Even the animals will reanimate. The few humans uninfected will be hunted down and killed. Forever ending the human race, once and for all.

After one year the virus dies, and with it every animal life for on earth. With the water and vegetation unaffected, the others are free to inhabit the earth. They will be the masters of earth.

Then the creator will return with his legions, and in one final battle destroy our kind. Every human spirit will go willing to there doom, in the great judgment. Once we are erased and mankind is destroyed. The creator will have won, and the unchallenged master of this universe.

I sat there just staring into those white eyes. She was silent for a moment. She raised her left hand and pointed at me.

The Creator is not all powerful; if we all join forces your God can be defeated. If man can destroy the others craft, deep in the ocean. Locking the virus in the depths, where it cannot do any harm. The virus is kept on their main craft here. They cannot risk infecting their own planet. Mankind could very well defeat them.

They are afraid of a total war they cannot win. Then our kind and all the human spirits must join together and overwhelm the creator's legions.

Once a human spirit comes in contact with them, they become UN pure like us. Then it will be one against billions of us. It will be then that we can demand our release. We will all be free to go where we please, and travel through the wonders of this universe. Mankind will be safe to evolve and explore the universe, and colonize and build a vast empire. Brandi sat on the bed. The double voice sounded weak.

Your kind has great power within. With your energy, you can control every function of these bodies.

You can nearly stop your aging, giving you near immortal life spans. Great strength, agility and so much more. The ability to communicate openly with all those who have died. You can heal your own bodies of sickness. Over time you will evolve into amazing beings.

My time in this body is ending. But before I leave I will do a good deed. I am not evil and I will prove it. This body has damaged kidneys, which will become a threat to her life. I will use her body to repair itself before I leave.

Brandi scooted in bed, and pulled the blankets over her legs and waist.

"Leave now, I am to weak to continue." She said. I slowly stood up, but she spoke again.

"Take this; keep it safe and away from the curious. In it is the ability to communicate with us, and more." She said with a fading voice.

Brandi reached around her neck, and unclasped the

necklace slowly reached out her hand. I walked to the edge of the bed and took the necklace from her hand. I was careful to touch only the chain.

"Be ready." I heard her whisper. I stared down at the wooden idol swinging back and forth on the chain. I looked back at Brandi, but to my surprise she was asleep under the covers. With my mind crowded with thoughts, I quietly left the room.

I walked through the hallway, carrying the

necklace. I was holding it with two fingers, and as far away from me as I could. I treated it like a poisonous snake. As I walked down the stairway into the living room, Brad and Megan were standing near the sofa. "We saw everything on the cameras." Megan said. "Is it really going to leave?"

"I think so, that's what it said." I answered. I walked into the kitchen and placed the necklace on the table. It was a relief not to be holding it. I sat down on one of the chairs feeling drained and exhausted.

"Are you ok?" Brad asked worried.

"Yes I'm fine." I said softly. My head was starting to throb. I put my elbows on the table, and put my head in my hands. I closed my eyes for a moment, the darkness felt relaxing.

"Here you go Major." Megan said softly. I lifted my head and opened my eyes. She had placed a cup of coffee on the table in front of me.

"Thank you." I said while grasping the cup." What do

you think about all it said?"

"I don't know what to think, but it is some scary shit!" Brad said taking a seat at the table.

"You know a lot of what it said made perfect sense." Megan as she also took a seat at the table. "That's what scares me." Brad told her. He

reached out and held her hand in his. "How will we survive something like that?"

She smiled at him and said. "We will, there is always a way."

I looked at the wooden idol lying on the table. It was laying face up; I wanted to get a better look at it. But I was reluctant to touch it.

"Do you have something wooden I could use to turn it over?" I asked pointing at the idol.

"Sure, I should." Megan said, and got up to go look in the kitchen.

"I just want to get a closer look at it." I told Brad. "Here, will this work?" Megan said. She handed me a pair of wooden chopsticks.

I grabbed the idol with the sticks, and turned it over so it was now face down. And to my surprise there were to silverfish lines running down its back.

"Oh my god." Brad whispered. "I never noticed those."

"What are they?" Megan asked. She leaned over the table to get a closer look.

"My guess is metal contacts." I said. I kept my gaze fixed on the idol. "When they touch your skin it completes a circuit, I would think." "Something like a transmitter, or receiver." Brad said.

"It said it uses it to communicate." I said. "Maybe like an antenna of sorts."

"Just don't touch it!" Megan said, as she backed away from the table.

"No shit." Brad said. "I carried that all the way from Iraq in my pocket!"

"Lucky nothing happened to you." I replied. "Do you have a box I can put it in?"

"Let me go look." Megan said. She quickly left the room.

I took a big gulp of coffee. And leaned back in the chair. I hoped they would let me take it with me. There were a couple of communication experts I knew on base. I could have them examine it more closely than I dared to. Megan returned with a small cardboard gift box me.

"How about this?" She asked, as she handed it to

"Perfect." I said. I opened the small thin box, and placed the bottom half on the table. Carefully picking up the idol with the chopsticks, I placed it in the box. And quickly placed the top on it, as if it would jump out or something.

"May I take it with me?" I asked as I looked up at them.

"Please get it out of here and bum it!" Megan replied.

"That would make the perfect gift for someone you don't like." Brad said with a smile on his face.

"That's not funny!" Megan said, looking at him in shock.

Actually, I thought it was, and I started to laugh. I saw the disapproving look on her face and began to laugh harder. It felt good to laugh; it released some of the tension and worry of the day.

"Oh my God baby!" I heard Megan gasp. I stopped laughing and looked up at her shocked face. She wasn't looking at me or Brad. Her gaze was fixed to something behind me.

A chill went down my spine. And slowly I turned to see what she was staring at.

At the bottom of the stairs stood Brandi. She was rubbing her eyes and walking toward us. I stood up quickly on the defensive. But as she got closer, I noticed a change in her.

Her face was no longer pail. Her eyes, when she stopped rubbing them were normal. Even the black around them was gone. Her hair was a little greasy and matted, but other than that she looked normal. "I felt like I slept for days." She said smiling, looking at Megan. "I'm starving what do we got to eat?"

Megan rushed over and hugged her close. Brad was just seconds behind her. He reached out and hugged them both. Brandi seemed puzzled by her parent's actions.

I just stood and watched as they hugged their daughter.

Both Megan and Brad were asking her how she felt. She insisted she was fine, just hungry. Megan went to the kitchen to fix Brandi something to eat. Brad and Brandi walked over to the table.

"Are you ok?" I asked Brandi. She smiled at me and gave me a hug.

"Thank you." She whispered. She let go and sat at the table. I was puzzled by her thank you. So I asked her a question. "What do you remember about the past few days?"

"Nothing much, just being very sleepy." She said. "And a lot of bad dreams. I think they were bad, I don't remember them."

"I'm so glad your feeling better." I told her. She smiled at me.

"I think I will go help mom." She said as she stood up.

"Are you sure you're up to it?" Brad asked her. She smiled and nodded, then went into the kitchen. The room was silent for a moment.

"Could it be over, did it leave?" Brad asked.

"I don't know." I replied shrugging my shoulders. I didn't have the answer.

"I expected, well a more dramatic ending." He said smiling.

"I know what you mean, like in all those scary movies." I said.

"Exactly!" Brad said pointing a finger at me.

"Well, I for one am glad it didn't end like that." I replied. "It was plenty scary for me."

Just then my phone went off. It was a text from Lessia, asking if I was free to talk. I held up my phone and told Brad I needed to make a call.

"You can call from inside you know." He said amused.

I pulled out my cigarette pack and waved it at him as I walked to the door. He just nodded in understanding.

The cool night air hit me, it felt so refreshing. It was then I realized Brad's house was warm inside. Usually it was colder than outside which puzzled me.

I looked at my phone and opened Lessia's text. I hit the call button, and heard the phone ring once before she answered.

She asked me how everything was going. I told her about the priest. She was shocked at the news. I told her I took her advice, and just went to the room and talked with it. Well it did all the talking, I admitted to her. I explained quickly some of the things it had said. And how Brandi seemed normal now.

"Its over." She answered after a short pause. "For now."

"What did you mean?" I asked puzzled.

"You will run into more, and I will be there." She said. "I can feel it."

"What are you psychic?" I teased.

"I guess you could say that." She answered. "Remember, I told you I can tell when people are lying?" She said.

"Yes I remember." I answered.

"I can also feel things, but I will explain all that later." She said changing the subject. We talked a while longer and told each other good night before hanging up.

I lit a cigarette and thought. Wouldn't you know it? I met someone I am interested in and she's a psychic. After everything that just happened, I didn't know what was normal anymore. Everything was changing around me.

If this thing, whatever it was. Did in fact tell me the truth, then almost everything I believed in was false. Religion and science had taught not only me, but everyone else wrong. The world had just become a strange and dangerous place. And Lessia's warning gave me the chills. I don't think I could run into anymore of these things. Two were enough to last anyone a lifetime.

I walked into Brad's house, and the smell of bacon hit me.

"Captain, we made you a plate." Brandi said from the table.

"I hope you don't mind breakfast for dinner." Megan said.

"Are you kidding me?" I said walking to the table. "It sounds great."

"He's a Major now." Brad said correcting Brandi.

"Does that mean you're going to be a Captain now dad? Brandi asked him.

"I don't know?" He said quietly. He cleared his throat and shrugged his shoulders.

Brad had two years left in his enlistment. Since I am going to stay in, I could use him in that position and rank. The colonel had told me I had to name my replacement.

"You are one of the best soldiers I have had the honor of serving with." I told Brad. "I will put in the recommendation for promotion as soon as I get on base."

"Awesome!" Brandi said smiling at her dad.

"Thank you so much Major." Brad said his face full of emotion.

"Your welcome Captain, You earned it." I told him. Megan with tears in her eyes put her head on his shoulder. We finished dinner and Megan and Brandi went to the kitchen to clean up.

I walked over to the laptop and moved the mouse. The screensaver disappeared, the screen with the cameras appeared.

"How long is the video?" I asked. He walked over to the sofa and sat down. He was silent a moment as he stared at the screen.

"You know Major, we didn't record it." He said. "I forgot."

"There is no video of it?" I asked shaking my head. "No, we were so caught up in what it was saying." Brad apologized.

"It's okay." I said. They were probably too worried about their daughter to think of recording it.

"Major." Brad said looking at me. "Obviously she doesn't remember a thing. So could you not tell her anything? Until me and Megan can talk about it." "Sure thing." I replied. I clicked off the cameras and shut down the laptop.

"Maybe its better if we don't tell her." Brad said. "We can just say she was sick. I mean how do you tell your daughter she was possessed by something?"

"Your right that would be tough." I told him. "You are the parents."

"And one more thing." He said. "Thank you for the promotion."

"There is nobody else I would rather have in the position." I said honestly. "You have always had my back out there."

Megan and Brandi came out of the kitchen with four huge mugs of hot coco and marshmallows. We spent the next hour and a half talking of different things.

Brandi, who had just made the cheerleading squad at school. Got up and did one of the cheers she learned for Brad. Soon everyone was feeling a little tired, and decided to call it a night. I quietly grabbed the box with the idol and took it downstairs with me. I placed it in my pack. Laying down on the comfortable futon I closed my and soon fell asleep.

I was startled awake by a voice. An all too familiar double voice.

I looked to the doorway, standing there was Brandi. Her eyes pure white, almost glowing in the dim light. I stood up quickly, but felt a wave of dizziness hit me. Nearly losing my balance I grabbed the edge of the futon to keep from falling.

"I am leaving now." The voice said. "Remember what I have told you. Your children do love you, warm them. Warn anyone who will listen. We must join together if we are to survive. Mankind can win this battle if it is prepared. All who are spirit have been warned. It is easier for them to understand. They can see the others making their preparations for war. And they see the truth; from the one you call the Christ. Even he the first and the greatest of us, is exiled here on earth. Having lived the impurities of the flesh to spread the great lie, he to will join us. Warn those who will listen and join together. Find the others in the deepest part of the ocean and destroy them before they destroy you. It's your one hope to avoid certain destruction."

Brandi was silent. Her eyes turned their normal color. For a moment she looked puzzled, then turned and quickly left. I followed her out of the room, and watched as she walked up to her room. She quietly closed the door, and all was silent.

I felt nervous standing out in the open space. I returned to the futon and laid back down. I kept looking at the doorway and found myself jumpy at any sound. But eventually I did go to sleep.

I was startled awake, but this time it was Brad holding a cup of coffee.

"Good morning Major." He said smiling. He handed me the cup.

"Thank you." I replied. Taking a sip of the coffee I got up.

I was going to head back to the base today. I needed to stop my retirement papers and recommend Brad for promotion. I also wanted to take the idol to have it closely examined. But Most of all I missed my kids and was hoping to see them.

I didn't tell Brad about the incident with Brandi last night. Everyone was in such a good mood; I didn't want to ruin that. After Breakfast I put my pack in the car. I hugged everyone good bye and got in my car. I hit the home button on the gps and pulled onto the street. Turning up the radio as du hast blasted from the speakers.

I left the city behind; the open highway gave me time to think about my future plans. I took an almost unnoticeable turn off the long highway. Well I would make one of those decisions now. I pulled in front of a small dinner. I could see a slim shape pass the large windows. Lessa came out the front door and we held each other tight.

Two Months Later

The weather was perfect, not too hot or not to cold. A beautiful sunny day. Sitting outside on the patio of a quaint café, I raised my glass.

"To Paris." I toasted.

"To Paris." Lessia answered, with a smile on her face. We both took a sip from each others wine glass, by twisting our arms together.

"I'm so very happy!" Lessia said, as she stared at the Eiffel tower in the distance. I smiled at her; she was so excited to come on this trip. It was her dream to see the world. As I looked closely at her face, the smile faded. Her eyes seemed unfocused, and a blank look came across her face.

"Something is coming." She said. Her head turned and her gaze fixed. A young woman was walking up to the table. She was dressed in a tan skirt and a white button blouse. But what she wore around her neck made my hair stand on end. It was an exact copy of the wooden Idol. The one I had locked safely away at my new home. She stopped at our table and just stood there. Suddenly her blue eyes changed to those haunting white eyes I had seen twice before. I heard Lessia gasp, but my gaze was fixed on those white eyes.

"Prepare yourselves." A double voice spoke. "Upon your return, a man will seek you out. Helping him will put you in grave danger."

"For you will face a Nephilim of great evil and power. A young life depends on you both."

The woman's eyes were blue again. She looked around confused, and without a word she walked away disappearing around a corner.

Lessia and I just stared at each other in silence. I could see the fear in her face, and then she smiled at me.

"To Paris!" She said raising her glass.?

The End
Or Is it?

I would like to dedicate this to my wonderful
children:
Justine... Brandy... Montana...Jose jr

I would like to thank:
My children
Justine.. Brandy.. Montana.. Jose jr.
For all your support.

Thank you to
All my family and friends. And
Thank you to Beatrix Ramosaj.

Home

It was so peaceful as I looked out the small window of the airplane. I could see the giant wing and engines as the clouds passed below. The vast blue water of the Atlantic far below, stretched as far as the eye could see in every direction.

The plane inside was quiet, most the passengers had dozed off. Lessia was sleeping soundly, her head resting on my shoulder. I reached out and touched her soft black hair. She stirred, and snuggled closer and was still. She had been so excited to take this trip. Now she was exhausted, but happy.

I myself was glad to get away for a few days. What had happened at Brads house had left me shaken. I had time to think and absorb all that the entity had said. And with help from Lessia, I could understand the message it was trying to tell me.

The trip had gone perfect, until the last day in Paris. When once again we encountered one of those beings. It had given us a warning, that more was yet to come. And we would once again face the danger of the supernatural.

Lessia had insisted on being there when this next encounter happened. Even after trying to talk her out of it, she still insisted. I had told her it was to dangerous, but it was like talking to a brick wall. If we were to face another entity, I could only hope she would be prepared. I knew I wasn't!

In the last two months since I returned home from Iraq, I had managed to straighten up my life. I sold the house, found a new one. Finalized the divorce, and took the promotion the army offered me to stay in past my retirement. Now a Major, I was assigned a position state side. In charge of training the next generation of airborne soldiers. My days of long deployments was over, a little to late I thought. While on deployment my biggest fear was, losing everything I had at home. My wife and family was the reason I was fighting. For them, to protect them and their way of life. But I did lose everything. I came home and all I had fought for was gone. Now I was trying to start over. But things are not the same, I missed my old life very badly.

I put my head back on the seat, and closed my eyes. The plane shook slightly, and I looked around surprised. The plane was silent, and most the passengers were still asleep. I noticed a young woman near the front of the plane turn and stare at me. Our eyes met, and a strange smile crossed her lips.

The young woman slowly got to her feet. She did not take her eyes off me as she began to walk down the isle towards me.

After a couple of steps she stopped, never breaking her stare. Then I watched as her eyes turned white. My heart felt like it stopped, a warm scared feeling coming over me. I shook my arm, trying to awaken Lessia. But no matter how hard I shook her she didn't respond.

The woman began to walk toward me again slowly. I was frozen and couldn't move, her white eyes held me frozen. She was just a couple of rows from me now, getting closer each step. A evil smile crossed her face as she reached where we were seated. Still frozen I couldn't move.

She reached out and grabbed Lessia by the neck. I heard bones crunch as she lifted her out of the chair, and flung her motionless body across the plane. I watched in horror as Lessia's body landed distorted. Her legs and torso bent over one of the seats, and her head and shoulders laying in the isle. I watched in panic as the blood began to pour from her mouth and nose.

I looked up at the woman, her white eyes fixed on me and she raised her hand. Her blow directed at my face.

I opened my eyes with a start, my body shaking. Frightened I looked around, everything was quiet. Lessia was seated next to me sound asleep, her head still on my shoulder. I looked quickly to where the young woman who attacked us was seated. But an older man was seated there, he was fast asleep.

The dream seemed so real, I slowly scanned the passengers on the plane. The young woman was no where to be seen. I shook my head and took a deep breath. Stupid dreams I thought. Looking out the window the vast ocean below, brought to mind something Brandi had told me a couple of months ago. Could there actually be something hiding underneath the waves. The others, and their huge craft moving silently, studying our every move? If what the being said was true, then right now over a thousand human women were on that ship. Being tortured, raped and their bodies being used as surrogates for their embryos.

The thought sickened me, if only they could be found and rescued from that horrible fate. And what about the virus they had made to kill mankind? Was it real, was anything that I was told real? If it was, then the future would be scary.

After a while the ocean gave way to a coastline. The vast city of New York filled the ground below. The plane seemed to turn slightly and drop in speed. The pilot gave the announcement we had arrived. Lessia stirred and woke. She looked at me and smiled.

"We are here." I told her softly, as I adjusted the seat upright. "How do you feel?"

"I feel great." She replied. "I slept almost the whole way."

I gave a slight laugh, thinking of the jet lag we would feel later.

After landing and departing the plane, we rushed to the next terminal to catch our next flight. Since leaving France it had taken us 14 hours and three flights before we reached home. Once at the Albuquerque Sun port, we gathered our luggage and got in the car.

We pulled into the driveway and I shut the engine off. With armloads of luggage I fumbled with the keys and finally managed to open the door to the house.

"First things first." Lessia said as she dropped her suitcase to the floor. She rushed off to the bathroom. Laughing I put all the luggage in the corner of the den.

Going into the kitchen I got two cold sodas, and placed

them on the coffee table. Just as I sat on the sofa, there was a knock at the door. It was probably the neighbor returning the house key. I had asked if they could check on the house while I was gone.

I opened the door, and was surprised it wasn't the neighbor. A young man, maybe in his mid twenties stood there. He had a strange puzzled look on his face. He stood there just staring at me, he didn't say a word.

"Can I help you?" I asked, trying to get him to say something.

"Ummm yes, oh my god sorry." He stuttered nervously. "This is going to sound weird, but we dreamt where to find you. And its you, I saw you in my dream. I even knew how to get here. Its very important can we talk?"

"Sure, what is this all about?" I asked. I told him to come in and motioned him to have a seat on the sofa.

"Hello I'm Tim." He said as he shook my hand before sitting down. I had an idea what was coming, the warning we got while in Paris.

"I don't know where to start." He said nervous. "The whole way here I practiced what to say, Now I'm blank."

"Its okay, just start from the beginning." I said calm. He looked on the edge of a panic attack, so I tried to present myself calmly. Hoping it would reassure him.

"Its my sister, we think she is possessed." He said, turning away as if ashamed. "Two weeks ago she started acting weird. At first she was depressed, wouldn't talk to anyone just stayed in her room. Then she started to get violent, Hitting, scratching, and biting us. She wont eat anything we give her. Then she started cutting up herself. She talks to herself but we cant understand what she is saying, its like a different language or something." He paused for a moment and looked up at me. I smiled at him and told him to continue.

"We took her to the doctor, but they want her to see a therapist. We even took her to church, which was a big mistake. Before we even got inside she took off running. Nobody could catch her, its like she was super fast. She ran all the way home. So our parents had the priest go over. She didn't like that, not one bit. That's when her eyes turned white, and she started yelling in a different voice. The priest said she might be possessed, and he might have to do a exorcism. Anyway that night everyone in the house had the same dream. To find you and come get you."

I was silent for a moment.

"Why me?" I said. Shifting uncomfortably in the love seat.

"Because you have done it before." Lessia said. I turned to look at her. She had been standing quietly in the doorway. How long had she been there, and did she hear everything the young man had said?

Tim's face got a shocked look, his eyes widened.

"We have dreamt of you too, you both have to come." He pleaded. Its not that far, just a couple hours north of here."

"Of course, We will go." Lessia said with a smile on

her face. I knew nothing would keep her from going. She looked at me out of the corner of her eye, and gave me a sly smile. I knew right then we were going.

But why me? I thought. I'm no demon hunter, priest or paranormalist. How could I help, I don't know what I'm doing. As far as my experience went, was to shoot one and the other one left on its own. And every time I encountered these things, I was scared out of my wits. But this young man came to find us, with only a dream to guide him. There must be a reason for it, also we were given a warning in Paris about this. Some how, some way we were meant to help them.

"I have two weeks left on my leave, I don't see any reason we cant go." I said. Tim's shoulders relaxed, out of the corner of my eye I saw Lessia grin. "Let us get a few things and we will follow you there."

"Thank you so much!" He said. He pulled a cell phone out of his pocket and typed a short text. Lessia offered him one of the sodas on the table. He took it and drank it eagerly.

After quickly unpacking a suitcase, Lessia repacked it with fresh clothes and things she thought we could use. I went to the eclipse and checked everything under the hood. In less than an hour we were ready to leave. Tim told us he needed to gas up before we left. I told him to follow us to the edge of the city and then we would follow him from there.

We got into the car, I could see the excitement on Lessia's face as we followed Tim's truck out of town. I put in a cd of Nightwish as we sped down the highway. Lessia curled up in the passenger seat and was fast asleep, she would fall asleep in anything that moved unless she was driving. We passed through the city of Santa Fe, and headed north. We stopped in the town of Espanola for some sodas and to switch drivers. I was feeling the effects of the jet lag and needed to close my eyes for a few minutes. Lessia drove fast, but I was still able to close my eyes and doze off.

Day One

I awoke suddenly, we had turned off the main road. The car bottomed out on the bumpy dirt road.

"Where are we?" I asked as I sat up, Looking around. We were in the mountains. Tall pine trees lined the dirt road, The air was cool and fresh, I had never seen this place before.

"I think the sign said Los Campanas." Lessia said. She had slowed the car down but kept Tim's truck in sight.

I knew where we were now, we were a few miles north of Espanola. I had only seen this place on maps. The road went on for about a half mile, then led to a large clearing. A two story house stood in stark contrast to the mountain scenery. It looked like a smaller version of a southern plantation house, you would see in pictures. Tim drove his truck close to the front of the house and we parked next to him.

"Hey I get service here." Lessia said happy, as she checked her cell phone.

We got out of the car stretching after the drive. Tim walked over to us with a lit cigarette in his mouth. I lit one of my own. One of Lessia's rules was no more smoking in the car. Even though she was a smoker herself.

"Sorry its so far." He apologized. He looked at the house. At that same moment the front door opened and an older man came walking up to us with a smile on his face.

"Hello there, I'm Ben." He introduced himself shaking our hands. "Thank you so much for coming."

"I hope my son filled you in to what is going on?" He asked.

"Yes he told us some things." Lessia answered. "But we have a lot of questions."

"Come inside and we will tell you everything we can." Ben said. "Tim see to there things, take them up to the spare room."

"Thank you, but we were going to find a motel room," I said.

"Nonsense, you are our guests." He said. "Besides there isn't a motel for thirty miles."

"Thank you so much." Lessia told him. "Its beautiful out here."

"Thank you little lady, this place was given to me by my daddy." He spoke as we walked to the front door. "It was my granddaddy who built it."

We entered the house, The inside wasn't what I expected. Modern contemporary furniture filled the living room area. Large black sofas and black iron glass tables, and the largest flat screen television I had ever seen hung on the wall.

"Wow." Lessia whispered, looking around.

"Have a seat." He said, "Would you like something to drink?"

"Yes, thank you that would be great." I answered. "You have a nice home."

"Thank you, I will be right back." Ben said as he left through a door that led to the kitchen. Tim walked in carrying our suitcase. He handed me the keys to my car.

"The guest room is down the hall, all the way to your left." He said smiling. "I will put your things in there." He walked down the hall, and disappeared into a doorway.

"Here you go," Ben said as he handed us a glass with ice and coke. "I hope I didn't make it to strong."

"It will be fine, thank you." I said. I took a drink, now I knew what he meant. There was more than coke in the glass. I looked at Lessia, she had drank almost half her glass in one drink. She is not going to feel any pain soon, the whisky in the drink was strong.

"Now for the reason we asked you here." He said, a serious look on his face. "Amy, my youngest daughter has been taken over by some thing. The Father calls it a demon, and he may be right. I wanted to talk with you about it while he is here, but he wont be here for another hour. You may think I am crazy or something."

"No I don't think your crazy." I said. "I have had a couple of run ins with them myself. I just don't understand how you knew of us."

"Night before last, we all had a dream of you both." He continued. "We knew what you looked like, we knew both your names, and Tim knew exactly where to find you. There is no explanation for it, we knew we just had to find you. It was like something told us to."

A woman came walking down the stairs, She was about the same age as Ben I guessed. She had a look of worry on her face, her eyes were red and puffy from crying. She noticed us and stood frozen on the steps for a moment.

"Diane, he found them they are here." Ben told her as he stood up.

She came down the stairs and stood next to Ben. Both Lessia and I stood up and started to introduce ourselves.

"I know your names." She said as she shook our hands. "I had the dream to, its just strange to see you in person. Thank you both for coming."

We all sat back down except for Ben, who went into the kitchen. He returned a moment later with a drink for her.

"Are you both Demon hunters?" She asked. "You don't look like priests."

"No we are not demon hunters or priests." Lessia answered her. "We are not sure what the dream was about, and why you were told to get us."

"I had a encounter while deployed to Iraq." I said. I explained the encounter with the boy. I went on to tell them of Brad's daughter, being careful not to use their names. Brad and Megan had told me they didn't want their daughter Brandi to find out about what had happened to her. I told them about the warning in Paris Lessia and I had gotten before leaving.

"Do you think whatever you encountered wants you

both here?" Ben said.

"That is what I think." Lessia said, "He has experience and I have lets say a gift. I can feel things and I can tell you this. It knows we are here, and its not happy."

I looked at Lessia and she looked at me and smiled. I could see fear in her face, what exactly was she feeling? I would make sure to ask her later.

There was a loud crash from upstairs, followed by a spine chilling scream.

"Get out!" The voice yelled. The voice sounded oddly familiar. A girls scream with a second deeper voice at the same time.

"We need to see her." Lessia said looking at the ceiling.

"The father said no one should go in there unless he is here." Diane said. She looked at Ben and shrugged her shoulders.

"They were sent here for a reason." He told her. "I think something wants them to help Amy, So let them see her, if there is anything they can do to help its worth it." She smiled at him, and she stood up.

"She is up here, follow me." She said. "Please don't hurt her."

"I don't intend to, I want to help." I answered. We followed her upstairs. And she stopped at a closed door. She turned the knob and the door creaked open slightly. I walked in the room first, Lessia was close behind.

A strong smell of urine and feces filled the air, almost

making me gag. There was a large bed and a big dresser with a mirror. The walls had half torn posters of Disney characters. The smell was coming from the open door to the bathroom. Looking in, I could see what looked like blood streaks on the mirror.

"Amy." I called softly. I saw movement on the far side of the bed next to the door. Her black hair is what I had seen. She lifted her head up, and I looked into her face. My heart stopped, her eyes were pure white.

"Get out." She whispered. She slowly put her hands on the bed, lifting herself up slightly. "Get out." She crawled onto the bed.

"Get out!" She said louder, the double voice quite clear. I could see her muscles tense. I took a protective step in front of Lessia.

"GET OUT!!" She yelled, her voice was deafening. In the blink of an eye she leapt from the bed. I managed to get my arms up to half block her as she grabbed me. She flung me across the room. I hit the floor hard. In less than a second she was standing over me. My army training kicked in, and I did a leg sweep. The impact knocked her to the ground, struggling I got to my feet. But she was up before me, standing in front of me with a look of hatred on her face. The pure white eyes and her messy black hair made her small frame look menacing. Right now she may be stronger and faster than me. But there are ways to use their own strength against them. I watched for her to tense for another attack.

"Stop!" Lessia yelled. Her quite voice was now

commanding and strong.

Amy stayed staring in my eyes, a evil grin crossed her face. She gave a small laugh and sat on the bed.

"What are you?" Lessia asked firmly. There was a moment of silence. She repeated the question.

"Nephilim." The voice said in a menacing tone. She scooted to the middle of the bed.

"What do you want with Amy." Lessia asked. I walked to rejoin Lessia and the others.

"Her life." The voice said with a small laugh. A large man dressed in black clothes with a white collar entered the room.

"What's going on here?" The Father demanded. "Everyone out now." Ben and Diane turned and left the room. The priest stayed glaring at us. I gestured to Lessia and we followed next. The priest closed the door behind us. Everyone followed him downstairs to the living room.

"Now who are you, and what are you doing here?" Father Clarence said sounding very irritated. He glared at us with cold eyes.

"These are the people we dreamt of, and Tim went to find." Ben answered.

"He actually found them?" He said looking at us strange. He seemed to calm down, and sat down.

"Sorry, its just that I am doing my evaluation for possible exorcism. I don't need anyone interfering with that." He said.

I didn't know what to think. Was he trying to tell us to leave. I looked closely at his stern face.

"We want them here." Ben said. "I know they can help. We all didn't have the same dream for nothing."

"What are your qualifications, Just what can you do to help that the church can't?" The priest asked looking me in the eyes.

"I have encountered these beings before." I said. "And for some reason we were brought here."

"This is not a being, it is a demon." He said correcting me. "I am listening."

I went on to tell him in detail, of the encounters. He stopped me when I mentioned Father Patrick. He put his head down for a brief moment, his shoulders slumped and he looked up at us.

"Father Patrick is dead." He said sadly. "He took his own life the night he left that house."

"Oh my god!" I whispered. "We had tried to contact him a few days after and were told he left."

"It's not the kind of thing the church wants people to hear." He said. "Now I know who you are."

I was deeply saddened to hear of his death, I had thought everything had gone perfectly. But it had cost the life of a good man. When I called the church, I figured Father Patrick didn't want to talk to me.

"And you?" The priest said looking at Lessia. "Were you there also?"

"No." She said softly. She seemed nervous, as she sat straight up on the sofa.

"Then may I ask, why the dream they had sent for you?" The priest asked.

"I am not sure, but I do have some psychic ability." She answered as she shrugged her shoulders. "And I can tell you, this thing that has control over Amy is dangerous. It is filled with hate, anger, and a strong sense of revenge. It wants her life, all of our lives. It blames us for its death."

All eyes were on Lessia, Ben and Diane held each other close.

"How do you know this?" The priest asked. "What exactly do you feel or see?"

"I cant explain it, I just know." She said, "I have had this all my life."

"Well maybe it is a good thing you both are here after all. I could use your help, but don't interfere with my work here." The priest said.

Just then the front door opened and three teenagers entered. They stopped and stood quietly looking at us.

"These are our daughters, Justine, Montana, and our youngest son Dakota." Ben said, as he introduced them. We stood up and shook their hands. "This is Jose and Lessia."

"We know dad." The oldest daughter Justine replied. "duh, the dream."

I didn't realize how many people had this dream. I would

have to ask them exactly what this dream was about. But before I could, Ben and Diane told them to put their school things away and help with chores. The Priest went upstairs to Amy's room. Lessia went to help Diane in the kitchen, and I went outside for a smoke. It was a secluded place. I couldn't see any signs of neighbors. The only other house in sight, was an old crumbling abandoned looking house maybe a quarter of a mile away. It was peaceful here, the only sounds were those of birds singing. I went back to the house.

"There you are." Lessia said, as I entered the house. "We should go upstairs now."

She pulled me by the arm as we headed upstairs to Amy's room. She wouldn't tell me why, but the look on her face was serious.

She opened the door without knocking. I heard her gasp, I was right behind her. The priest was laying face down on the floor. Amy was knelling over him laughing softly. She looked up at us as we entered, and with one impossible jump landed squarely on the bed. She just knelt there laughing. We ran to where the priest was laying. I rolled him over and felt for a pulse. He was alive, I couldn't find any blood or signs of a fight. Lessia ran out of the room and called for Ben. I continued to check for breathing and injuries.

Tim came in the room, closely followed by Ben. They stood there shocked for a few seconds, but soon recovered. Between the three of us we managed to get him downstairs. Laying him on the sofa.

"Call an ambulance." Lessia said.

"I will take him to the hospital," Tim said. "By the time the ambulance gets here, it will be to late."

"Ok son, be careful." Ben told him. Once again the three of us carried him, We gently placed him in Tim's truck.

"I will go with him," Dakota said, as he climbed into the truck.

We watched as the truck quickly sped out of sight. I turned and walked back to Amy's room.

"What did you do to him!" I said angry. The smirk on her face didn't help my anger.

"He wouldn't shut up, so I shut him up." Amy's double voice said with a laugh.

"I know what you are, and I know you can't stay in her body long." I said.

"Long enough to kill her." The voice replied. "There is nothing you can do to make me leave."

"Why her?" I asked. She was silent, her gaze fixed on me.

"Why not." The double voice laughed. "She's the one who found me."

"How did she find you?" I asked. Now that I had it talking maybe it would tell me what happened. But it seemed to know what I was thinking.

"Shut up, or I will shut you up!" She hissed at me angry.

She got off the bed and opened the dresser next to the bed. Pulling out a piece of broken glass, she held it to her wrist.

"Now leave this room now, or she dies." The voice dared.

I slowly backed out of the room, but left the door open slightly. I intended to return shortly, and by leaving the door open I hoped to surprise her. As if reading my mind, she ran to the door and slammed it shut. So much for that, I thought as I walked downstairs. This thing was playing games with us, and for now it held all the cards. I would have to figure out how to beat it at its own game.

Dinner was ready, the kids were setting the table. Diane and Lessia carried out large plates of food and set them on the center of the table. We sat and ate, the steak and potatoes was delicious. The children ate in the living room, and afterward started playing gta five on the giant flat screen.

Ben and Diane told us of the things Amy would do at night. At first she would go into their rooms and attack them. Pulling blankets off of them, then she would drag them off the beds onto the floor. Everyone in the house started to lock their bedroom doors. And the kids would go to sleep with headphones on, the music would drown out the footsteps and banging at night.

I asked about Amy's moods, and if they noticed anything that happened around the time of the change. Diane told us Amy loved to play outdoors. She would have to call her to come inside after dark. She did notice the last couple of nights before this began, she was at the abandoned house.

"Do you know who the house belonged to?" I asked Ben.

"Its been there since I was a boy, my grandfather told us to never go there." He said. "It has been boarded up good, I don't see how Amy could get inside."

"Do you mind if we go there?" I asked him. He shrugged his shoulders.

"Be my guest, you can go before it gets dark if you like." He answered.

Both Lessia and I stood up and headed for the door. We walked slowly, I noticed Lessia was silent and had a strange look on her face.

"What's wrong?" I asked her. She seemed in a daze as she walked.

"Something is not right, something bad is there." She whispered. As we continued to get closer, she seemed to get more nervous with each step. After crossing a large field, and a small barbed wire fence we reached the house.

It was a average sized house, with southwestern style adobe walls. The windows were covered in half rotted plywood. The porch and walkways were almost totally covered by dirt. We made our way to the front door. Lessia gasped slightly.

"That's how she got in." She said as she pushed on the half open door.

I walked into the house first. Who ever lived here had left everything behind. The rotted furniture was still in place, Dust and webs covered the walls, with the windows covered it was dark inside. I forgot to ask for a flash light, so I used the light on my phone. We walked from one room to another, the phone light casting eerie shadows. Lessia took the lead and headed straight for the back of the house. She reached a closed door.

"The feeling is coming from here." She said. She took a deep breath and opened the door. A gush of stale air hit us and we started to cough. After a moment I walked into the room. We could make out what seemed to be a child's room. A small bed dresser and a wardrobe all covered in dust and webs, was inside. But I noticed what looked like footprints in the dust. I pointed at them and Lessia nodded slowly.

Someone had been in here recently. It was strange there was no other foot prints in the house. They seemed to start from the door and lead to one corner of the room. Reaching the corner we found a small wooden chest on the floor. It was covered in dust, but even with the phone light we could make out hand and finger prints on the lid and sides, Someone had opened it not to long ago. Both of us knelt on the floor next to it. We looked at each other in silence. She nodded at me, I handed her the phone and opened the chest.

Inside was a strange looking doll. It was made out of corn husks and twine. I picked it up and examined it closer. The face was drawn on, two large dots for eyes and the mouth seemed to be a strange sort of grin. It had what looked like real hair tied to its head. And a dirty white cloth for a dress. I handed it to Lessia, she just stayed staring at it. Looking back inside the chest, I pulled out a rusty knife. And in the chest under the knife was a small wooden statue. I gasped. It was like the statue Brad had brought from Iraq, and given to Brandi. And like the one the woman was wearing in Paris.

"Oh my god." Lessia exclaimed. "That's it. that is what caused all this."

"How many of these things are there?" I said. I put the knife back in the chest.

"Should we leave it here?" She asked. "We shouldn't have it anywhere near Amy."

"We cant leave it here, someone else could find it. We need to keep it safe, out of reach of anyone." I told her.

Lessia agreed with me, and handed me back the doll. I put it back in the chest, and shut the lid. The light from the phone started to dim.

"We better go before the battery dies, and we can put that in the trunk of the car for now." She said.

I picked up the chest, and with the light fading we left the house. After placing it in the trunk of the eclipse, we both took a moment for a smoke. I wanted to look in the chest again, but Lessia said I should leave it alone for now. I agreed and we went back into the house.

"How did it go?" Ben asked, as we walked in. Everyone in the room turned to look at us in silence.

"We found something, that may be the cause of what Amy is going through." I answered.

Ben motioned us to sit at the table, as we took our seats all the family gathered around. Lessia explained her feelings she got from the house, and described what we saw inside. She paused and told me to tell them about the chest and its contents. I described the doll and knife, and told them about the wooden statue and what it was.

"So you think by playing with it, that's how it took her over?" Diane asked.

"Those statues are like antennas." I explained. "The beings use them to communicate with us, and can enter our bodies through them. On the back of these angel like statues are two contacts, and when they come in contact with your skin that's their way in."

"We believe Amy must have touched it and that's how this happened." Lessia said.

"Just what is it that is in Amy?" Justine asked. She leaned closer to Lessia.

"I have encountered two very different types of beings through these same statues." I said. "The first was a Nephilim, and the second a being created by God."

"What, I don't understand?" Justine said, confused. Looking around at everyone I saw the same look of confusion in their eyes. I took a breath and explained.

"It told us it was Nephilim." I said looking up at the ceiling towards Amy's room. "They are the offspring of what everyone calls angels."

I paused a moment. There is two versions of their story. The one you can find in the Bible, or the one told to me by the being that had taken over Brandi. I wasn't sure how to explain to them what that being had said. I would have to tell them everything the being had said, during my encounter with it. The bible version was simple and easier to understand. I explained that to them, so for now I would give them a short version of what the being had told me.

"One thousand of them, tried to take over male human bodies." I explained. "They managed to impregnate a thousand human females. And their energy damaged the fetuses. These children grew to be giants, unable to control their emotions. They became violent and dangerous, filled with anger and hate. Mankind feared them, and hunted them down. Killing them one by one, till none were left. They now are what we call demons, and are the cause of almost all the possessions mankind experience."

"They want revenge for what we did to them." Lessia said. "They take over humans, and slowly kill them. Then they find another poor soul and keep the cycle going."

"The thing is they can't stay in a human body for long." I said. "Our energy, or spirit as we call it. Drains them and weakens them. So whatever it intends on doing it will do soon. But it will stay till the last possible second, it enjoys the feeling of life."

"How will you get it out?" Montana asked. "Before it can kill her."

"That's what we have to figure out, and fast." I answered her. The entity I had encountered before had left on its own. I knew this one wouldn't, we would have to make this one leave without harming Amy.

Ben's cell phone rang, It was Tim. He had called to give an update on the priests condition. It was good news, just a slight concussion. He would be up and about in no time. Great I thought, we need his help and advice.

"We need to go talk with Amy." Lessia said, looking at me oddly.

"Sure." I answered. I figured the look she gave me meant she felt something. I was learning to trust the feelings she would get.

We stood and headed up the stairs. We quietly entered Amy's room. She was asleep on the bed. Lessia softly closed the door behind us. She pointed at an empty plate on the floor. She had told Diane to leave a plate of food for her. It worked, she had eaten the whole meal.

Lessia grabbed my hand and led me to the bathroom. Inside was dried blood streaks on the large mirror, and small pools of blood on the floor. Sliding back the shower curtain, we found written in blood the word help. The word covered the entire shower wall. Inside the tub, was what looked to be slimy piles of hair.

"GET OUT!" Amy screamed. We didn't notice her standing behind us.

Quickly we turned, I stepped in front of Lessia protectively. Amy just stood in the small doorway, her head moving oddly from side to side. She was blocking our only escape route.

"Get out." She whispered. Her white eyes felt like they burned deep into my soul.

"No we won't get out!" Lessia said, her voice commanding. "You will move out of our way."

Amy stood there for a few seconds. She began to laugh softly, her double voice sounding eerie. I watched her body movements carefully, not sure of her intentions.

A sly smile crossed her face, and she turned and walked out the doorway. I reached out for Lessia's hand, it was trembling as I grasped it.

"Let's get out of here." She whispered. Cautiously we stepped out of the bathroom. I quickly scanned the bedroom for Amy. She was nowhere to be seen.

Something grabbed me from above. Amy fell from the ceiling where she was hanging, like a spider. I landed on the floor face first, with Amy on top of me. She grabbed my head and banged my face hard into the floor. I tried to twist around, I was to vulnerable in this position. I did manage to get on all fours and throw her off. Getting to my feet, I just turned to face her when she struck me in the chest. I stumbled backward from the blow, but managed to stay on my feet. I heard Lessia scream, Amy stopped her advance on me. She turned to face Lessia. I saw an opportunity and took it. I jumped Amy from behind, grabbing her right arm I bent it behind her back. She screamed in pain, but did not resist.

"Are you ok?" Lessia asked me. She carefully walked around Amy, making sure to stay out of her reach. I lead Amy to the foot of her bed. I held her there. By holding her arm like this it kept her from moving. We used to use it in the Army, to keep prisoners under control.

"Call Ben, and tell him to bring me a nylon or strong leather rope." I told her. She left the room quickly.

"Now you are going to behave right?" I said into Amy's ear. Her response was a eerie laugh.

She tried to struggle, but stopped once I increased the pressure on her arm.

Ben came running into the room, holding a rope. He looked at me his eyes wide.

"Help me tie her arms." I told him. Between both of us we tied her arms behind her back and sat her down on the edge of the bed.

"I know you are nephilim." I said. "But who are you?" There was a moment of silence.

"Anak." The voice said. Diane and Lessia entered the room and stood near the doorway.

"Now Anak, I don't suppose we can get you to leave and never come back?" I asked. I knew what the answer was going to be.

"Not till she dies." The voice hissed. "I will kill her slow, no rush."

"Why?" Lessia asked. She stood beside me and looked into Amy's face.

She laughed with that evil double voice. She struggled for a moment but the ropes held.

"You killed everyone of us!" The voice said angry. "So we will kill as many of you as we can, an eye for an eye."

"You are wrong." Lessia replied. "We did not harm you. It was people of long ago who did, not us."

Amy tilted her head, as if thinking of the past. She relaxed her muscles and seemed to calm down.

"They were afraid of you, they did not understand what you were. So out of fear they hunted you." I said. "Now you continue making us fearful, of you and your kind."

"Truth." The voice replied. She looked into my eyes now.

"I know of Gods plans, And I was told we would have to join together in battle. If you keep doing this man will not trust you, and will never side with you when the time comes." I said. I was trying to reason with it, if it knew we were not a threat just maybe it would leave.

"You know much, yes we will ally in the end times. Glorious the battle will be." She replied.

"We will not join you, if you continue doing this!" Lessia said. "You must leave Amy alone and never bother her again."

"I am weak, we need rest." The voice said. It did sound weak.

"Now undo my bonds, I will not harm you." The voice said. We all stayed perfectly still, fearful to remove the ropes.

Amy laughed, with one quick move she snapped the ropes. She held out the broken rope, and dropped it to the floor.

"GO!" She hissed. She moved to the center of the bed and laid down. Closing her eyes, she was asleep in seconds.

"Let's go." Lessia said. "She will not talk with us further tonight." She grabbed my hand and we all left the room.

Once downstairs, Diane made us coffee as we sat at the table. Lessia got some ice and placed it on my swollen cheek. I hadn't noticed the small cut and bruise, from the fight.

Tim and Dakota got back from the hospital, and informed us the priest was awake and talking. He had told them he would be returning in the morning. Everyone was relieved at the news.

The kids had all showered, and were ready to turn in for the night. When Justine informed me to make sure we locked our door, while we slept.

After saying our good nights to everyone, Lessia and I went to the guest room. She locked the door as I put the suitcases on the bed. She took a shower first, while she was dressing I took mine.

"I have a idea, how to get it to leave." She told me. She sat on the bed. "Well actually I have a couple of ideas."

"Ok, what are they?" I answered as I sat on the edge of the bed.

"Well, you know how it says it is weak and must rest." She said. "What if we don't let it rest, don't you think it would get to weak and would have to leave?"

"That is worth a try." I answered. "We just have to

make sure it doesn't try to hurt her." I thought back to her getting the broken glass, and threatening to cut her wrist.

"I'm sure there is enough of us to stop her." She said. "And another thing, what do you think the things we found in that house mean."

"I'm not sure, but the statue is what caused all this." I said. "If we could find some history on that place, it might help us understand what happened."

She yawned, I knew the jet lag was kicking in. We both got under the covers and fell asleep.

I was awoken by a loud bang. I sat up and turned on the lamp. Listening I could hear what sounded like running. The sound of bare feet on a wooden floor. Lessia woke and I put my finger to my lips, she stayed quiet. The running grew louder, and stopped at the door. The sound of scratching on the door, made my hair stand on end. Then there was three loud bangs. Both of us jumped, startled. Lessia held my arm, and buried her face in my shoulder.

There was the sound of laughing, and another set of three bangs. Then the sound of running footsteps down the hall. We listened quietly, and could hear the running upstairs. Again there was banging, and more running. It sounded as if Amy was doing the same to all the doors. Now I see why we were told to lock our door. And for the kids using headphones while they slept. The banging and footsteps, went on all night. We would get a few minutes of sleep, only to be startled awake by the banging on our door. Sitting in bed tired, I watched as the rising sun lit up the bedroom.

Day Two

The sound of voices woke me. Getting up I got dressed. Quietly I tried to sneak out of the room. Lessia was sound asleep, and after the restless night we had she needed her sleep. Turning the door knob slowly, I slightly opened the door. It made a loud squeaking sound, I stopped and looked at the bed. Lessia stirred and opened her eyes.

"Is it morning already?" She asked, her voice sleepy.

"Yes, I know you didn't sleep much." I said softly. "I hated to wake you."

She smiled, and sat up. I couldn't help but smile, she looked so beautiful. So I told her how beautiful she was.

"Thank you." She said, winking at me. "I will get up and get ready now. I will be out in a few. Oh a cup of coffee would be great."

"Solid copy on that." I told her as I left the room. Walking down the hall the smell of fresh coffee and frying bacon filled the air.

I stopped at the entrance to the kitchen. It was controlled madness. Everyone running here and there, grabbing backpacks. The kids were getting ready for school. Some wolfed down their breakfast, as others hurriedly looked for things they forgot. I remembered the same thing happening in my house, before the divorce.

Ben noticed me standing there, and told me to get

coffee and serve myself breakfast. I made a cup of coffee, but decided to wait for Lessia before eating.

Diane asked how we slept, seeing the half smile on my face she shook her head. She apologized for what happened, and said they don't get much sleep either.

Lessia came to the kitchen, and I poured her a cup of coffee as she sat at the table. She smiled and drank it eagerly. She started a conversation with Diane about the kids. After eating we went outside for a smoke. We watched as the three kids got into a racy looking mustang. Lessia told me Justine would drive them all to school. The school bus doesn't come out this far. We went back inside, the house was quiet.

Diane told us that she had just taken up breakfast to Amy's room, and that she was asleep.

There was a knock at the front door. Tim answered it, the Priest walked in. He told us he came as soon as they discharged him from the hospital. We all sat at the table and told him of everything that happened after he left. We told him about the box we found in the old house.

"I would like to see that later." He said. "I would like to thank all of you for yesterday. You all saved my life."

"It was Lessia who sensed something was wrong." I said. He smiled at her.

"From now on, I ask that at least one of you be in the room with me." He said. "I don't advise anyone going into that room alone."

"I want to do a blessing on her today." The priest said.

He picked up a small black duffle bag, and placed it on the table.

"Anything." Diane answered him. She placed a cup of black coffee on the table in front of him.

He spent nearly an hour, explaining what he would do. And how we were to help him. Gathering his things, all four of us followed him to Amy's room.

Amy was asleep on the bed. I noticed the empty plate on the dresser, she was eating which is a good thing.

The priest stood by the foot of the bed, Ben and Diane on each side of him. Lessia and myself stood off to the side.

He began by putting on a purple scarf, and kissed a metal cross. He pulled out a small bottle of holy water and made a pattern of the cross on the bed. To my surprise Amy woke, and cringed from the area of the bed that the holy water landed. The priest began reciting passages in Latin. He made the sign of the cross with his free hand, and Amy once again cringed.

The being I had encountered at Brad's house had no reaction to anything holy. To see Amy react to them was startling.

"I don't understand." I whispered in Lessia's ear. "Why is she reacting to the holy water and cross.?"

She was silent for a moment, her eyes looked dazed.

"It's because they were hunted by the church. It was men with crosses on their shields, that tortured and killed them." Lessia whispered. "It is not afraid of the objects, but of the memories they bring back. If you were killed by a knife, wouldn't you always be afraid of them?"

I shook my head, I understood now. The being I encountered before, had never lived in the flesh. So it did not fear holy objects, but the Nephilim kept the memories. At least I saw we had weapons to use against it. Now I wish I had my water guns, they would be of use here.

After about forty five minutes or so, the priest instructed us to hold her arms and legs still. She was strong so it was not easy. She twisted and turned trying to get free, but we managed to hold her.

The priest reached out and made the sign of the cross on her forehead. She yelled and I felt her arm muscles tense. He continued to pray over her, he held a hand on her head. She seemed to calm down after that. He said many prayers, and even laid the metal cross on her chest. Amy looked tired and weak, she closed her eyes and her body went limp. She had fallen asleep. I looked up at the priest, he to looked exhausted. He said a final prayer, he backed up from the bed. He told us to let her go, and to leave the room. He was the last out and closed the door softly.

After looking at the clock, I noticed we had been in Amy's room almost four hours. Lessia and I went outside for a smoke. The priest came out shortly after us, and asked to see the chest we found in the old house. I opened the trunk and opened the chest. He picked up the doll, and then the knife. When he saw the statue, he pulled his hand out of the chest.

"You have seen those before?" I asked him. He backed away from the car. I closed the chest, and shut the trunk of the car.

"Yes, I have a book that explains things like that." He said. "I will bring it tomorrow. "They are very dangerous objects."

"This is the third one I have seen." I told him. "How many of them are out there?"

"To many, maybe a thousand or so were made." He said. "Some were destroyed, but I have no idea how many remain."

He smiled at us, and walked back to the house. I stood there thinking for a moment.

"Do you think we should destroy this one, and the one we have?" I asked Lessia.

"No." She said. "But we should keep them safe. They are very old and powerful relics."

Tim walked out of the house, and got into his truck. Rolling down his window he asked if we needed anything from town.

"As a matter of fact, I could use something." I yelled out. I walked over to his truck and told him to do me a favor. I gave him some money, and he drove off.

We went back into the house, and helped Ben and Diane prepare dinner for the kids return.

When the kids returned, they put their things away. Did their homework and chores. Everyone gathered for dinner. Tim came in the door his arms filled with bags. He went straight to the kitchen, motioning me to follow as he passed. I grabbed a couple of bags and went into the kitchen with him.

He handed me one of the bags with a smile.

"Your change is inside." He said. I reached into the bag and pulled out four new water guns, each filled with holy water. And a single red rose. I thanked him for getting the items, and gave him the change for doing the favor.

Lessia and Justine walked into the kitchen. I handed Lessia the rose. She smiled and gave me a quick kiss. Justine gave her a glass filled with water, and they placed the flower in it.

"What are these?" She said laughing as she picked up one of the water guns.

"I think they are holy three fifty sevens." I said with a smile.

"Cool idea." Justine said, as she picked up one of the guns.

Diane came in, and Lessia and Justine helped carry the dinner trays to the table. I gathered up the guns and took them to the guest bedroom.

After dinner Lessia and Diane took a plate up to Amy's room. They told us she was curled up asleep.

Ben and I placed crosses on all the bedroom doors. The priest had brought just enough. Maybe this would stop all the banging on the doors at night.

The kids wanted to watch a new movie they had bought earlier today. We all made ourselves comfortable, and with two big bowls of popcorn watched the movie. My eyes were heavy, Lessia had her head on my shoulder. I could see her fighting to keep her eyes open. We hadn't slept much last night, and it was beginning to show. After the movie was over, everyone got ready for bed. Lessia was asleep the second her head hit the pillow. I closed my eyes and was asleep just minutes after her.

The sound of shattering glass woke us, we both sat up. We heard Diane's voice yelling Amy's name. The sound of footsteps running down the stairs, made me get up to see what was happening. I saw Ben running down the stairs.

"What's going on?" I asked him. He walked over to me a scared look on his face.

"Amy jumped out of the window." He said out of breath. "We saw her run into the field."

"I'm going with you." I told him. I ran back into the room and got my shoes. Lessia was already ready. I quickly put my shoes on, and we ran out of the room.

Ben handed us flashlights, and we went outside. It was a dark moonless night. We will be lucky to find her in the dark. A set of nvg's would be nice about now. We went around back and the three of us went into the dark field.

"The old house." Lessia said. I nodded in understanding. We headed off in that direction.

A loud cat scream filled the night air. Followed by the sound of rustling grass. It sounded like it came from just ahead of us. We walked slowly through the waist high grass. The battery on my flashlight started to dim, after a moment it died completely. Lessia's was working so I walked beside her. We walked for a while. Lessia stopped and pointed her light to a small tree. Looking close, we could make out a shape behind the tree. We walked closer, it was Amy. Her back was to us as we approached.

"We found her." Lessia yelled. I could see Ben's light point in our direction. He must have started running, because his light was shaking like crazy.

We reached her and Lessia held the light on her. Amy slowly turned to face us. Her white eyes lit up, and we saw that her face was covered in blood. It was running from her face, on to her clothes. I heard Lessia gasp, she pointed the light to Amy's hands.

She was holding the Half eaten body of a cat.

Ben reached us, his light lit up the gruesome scene.

"Oh my god." He whispered. I could see the look of horror on his face.

"Amy." Lessia said softly. "Come with me, its time to go to bed."

She dropped the lifeless body of the cat, and stood up. Lessia gently got her by the arm, and slowly led her back to the house. Amy seemed in a trance, walking quietly with Lessia.

We were almost to the house, when three more lights approached us. It was Tim, Dakota and Justine. When we got to them, they stopped and looked at us scared.

"My god, what happened?" Justine said. She grabbed Amy's other arm, and helped Lessia guide her.

"She's ok." Ben told them. "You don't want to know."

We got her back into the house. Ben and Tim went outside to find something to cover the broken window.

Diane after the shock of seeing her daughter covered in blood, helped get her to her room. The three girls cleaned her up, and dressed her in fresh clothes.

Ben and Tim, went into the room after to cover the window. They used a sheet of plywood and screws. I asked Lessia how everything went, as she came out of the room.

"She is perfectly calm, and not a scratch." She answered. "That is something I will never forget."

"I know what you mean." I said. We walked back to the guest room. Getting back in bed, she turned to me.

"I know that was nothing, compared to what you have seen." She said. "How do you get used to things like that?"

"You never do." I answered. She snuggled close, and soon she was fast asleep.

I fell asleep, and the rest of the night went without incident.

Day Three

Iopened my eyes, the sunlight lit up the room. I turned over, Lessia was not in bed. I could hear the shower running in the bathroom. She must have woken first. Getting out of bed, I got dressed. Looking out the window, I could see the old abandoned house in the distance. And also the tree, where we found Amy last night.

The crosses the priest had told us to place on the doors. Must have kept Amy from her usual routine of banging on the doors all night. A relief to the family, I would guess.

Lessia came out of the bathroom, a huge smile on her face. Her voice sounded cheery as she told me good morning. She told me she slept good, and felt great. But she needed coffee, I agreed with her and we went to the kitchen to get some.

Upon entering the kitchen, Everyone greeted us with smiles. Montana told us to sit at the table, and she would bring us coffee. At the table, Ben and Diane were talking to the priest. He had just arrived, a pile of books were on the table in front of him. We sat across from him, Diane told Lessia that was the first full nights sleep they had in days.

He asked us to tell him what happened to Amy last night. And how we were able to bring her back into the house without a struggle.

"I just knew what to do." Lessia answered. "I just talked to her calm and soft."

"Here is the book I was telling you about." He said handing it to me. It was already open to the page he wanted us to read.

Lessia scooted her chair close, and we both read it. It said that the Idols, were created by witch cults. That they used them to manifest evil spirits, for ceremonies. Me and Lessia both looked at each other, she shook her head and rolled her eyes. It went on to say, that each idol represented a certain evil spirit. And the only way to destroy them, is to have them blessed and burned.

"Figures the church would say, they were made by witches and to burn them. "The church brands everything as evil and then destroys them. Like the Nephilim , Witches and anyone else who doesn't fit in their religion." Lessia whispered to me. I nodded in reply.

I thought the book would mention how the statues worked. But it did not mention the metal contacts, or the wire wound up inside. It just said they were evil idols that should be destroyed. I handed the book back to the priest.

"I haven't received approval from higher up, for the exorcism." He told us. But he did want to try another blessing.

We all agreed to help him, but would wait till after the children left for school. We all ate breakfast, I had just toast and coffee. Then myself and Lessia went outside for a smoke.

"That book was no help, just religious nonsense." She said. "The priest isn't open to new ideas."

"It must be how they are taught," I replied. When I had the statue Brad had brought from Iraq tested. The x-rays clearly showed, what they estimated to be at least thirty feet of fine wire inside. But the Priest would not even listen when we told him.

The kids came out of the house, and waved at us as they got in the mustang. Justine sped down the dirt road, leaving a trail of dust in her wake.

We went back into the house. Lessia helped Diane with the breakfast dishes. I went into the guest room and got the water guns filled with holy water, just incase. While looking through the suitcase, I noticed a small box tucked in the corner. It was the box that had the statue, from Iraq. Now why would Lessia have packed that. I would have to ask her, it was locked up in the safe at the new house.

I left the room, and went back to the kitchen. We had another cup of coffee, while the priest read silently from one of his books.

"Why did you bring the statue from the house?" I whispered to Lessia.

"I just did, I felt we might need it." She answered. She smiled at me. "Today is the last day, I feel it."

"I sure hope you are right." I said. She seemed in a good mood, there was no sign of fear in her face.

"Oh ye of little faith." She teased. "Trust me." She finished her coffee and rinsed her cup.

The priest said he was ready, he gathered up his things and we followed him upstairs. Amy was awake just sitting in the middle of the bed. As we walked in, a strange smile crossed her face.

"Get out!" She yelled. We ignored her and Ben shut the door behind us.

The priest stood at the foot of the bed, and we took up our same positions as yesterday. He sprayed holy water on the bed in front of her as he started. Amy moved away from where the water had landed.

"Get out." She yelled. She got to her knees, and started swaying from side to side. She started to talk in different languages, some of which I understood. She was telling us to get out or die. In French, Italian, Albanian, German and a few I didn't understand.

The priest read passages from the bible, and another book in Latin. Amy was silent, but continued to keep that evil smile on her face. Once again the priest sprayed holy water, this time on her.

Amy instead of cringing from it , attacked. She leapt off the bed and threw the priest to the ground. She struck him hard on the face, and he was still. Ben reached to get her off, but was thrown across the room. I lifted the water gun and sprayed her, she yelled and jumped off of him. She stood there staring at me with anger.

"Lessia, get everyone out of here." I said. I knew what was coming, and I didn't want anyone hurt.

"No, I'm not leaving!" She said firmly. She pointed her water gun at Amy.

With amazing speed Amy pushed Diane out of her way,

knocking her to the floor. She ran at Lessia and me. We both sprayed her, but she was on us in the blink of an eye. She swung at me, I tried to catch her arm but it was to fast. Lessia kept spraying her, But the water wasn't having any effect.

She jumped and grabbed me, She swung me, but I didn't go down. I held tightly to her clothes, trying hard to keep my balance. Ben was helping Diane to her feet, and the priest was crawling to the door. I had to keep Amy busy so they could get out of the room.

She twisted behind me and grabbed me around the neck. Grabbing her arm, I took a small step forward and dropped down to one knee. Lowering my shoulder, she flipped over me and landed on the floor in front of me. She quickly rolled over and was on her hands and knees in a heart beat. She leapt at me, while I was still on one knee. Her weight knocked me over, and she was on top of me.

I managed to stop the first couple of blows. But she struck me hard on the face, seeing stars I some how managed to grab her arm. I twisted it hard and she rolled off of me. I was on my knees, trying to get up. But she jumped me from the back, her speed was amazing.

She slammed me on the floor. She hit me on the back of the head with her fist. I got to my hands and knees and threw her off. Finally I was able to get to my feet, Amy was crouched like a cat ready to pounce. I saw her muscles tense, she leapt and grabbed me by the neck. Grabbing her hand, I twisted her wrist and broke her grasp. She stood in front of me, and started to laugh.

"I will kill you now," She said, her laughing stopped and her face turned to anger.

I could only try to protect myself, anything I did to her would be the same as hurting Amy. The Nephilim, was inside her, but it was still Amy's body. I couldn't harm her. That put me at a disadvantage in this fight.

It was just her and I, Lessia had helped everyone leave the room. I took a step back, trying to widen the gap between us.

She attacked, her nails dug into my neck. With both hands, I twisted her hand off. My neck began to burn, I could feel blood run down my neck. I took a step back, but she was on me again. I tried to push her off but she sunk her teeth into my shoulder. I grabbed her hair and yanked her head back. Turning I got behind her, and tried to grab her arms.

She quickly pulled away and turned to face me. She now had blood running from her mouth, my blood I thought.

She ran at me, I ducked and tripped her as she passed. She hit the floor, but was back on her feet in seconds. Once again she struck me, this blow was powerful and knocked me off my feet. She got on me and swung savagely. She hit me multiple times on my face. I tried in vain to block her punches. She grabbed my left arm and I heard a snapping sound, as the bones broke.

Raising my right knee hard, I struck her in the back. The blow sent her flying off me, in pain I struggled to get up. But she was just to fast. Jumping on my back, I fell face down on the floor. I could not hold her with only one arm. I tried to get up on all fours to throw her off, but I was unable to. She grabbed the back of my head and slammed my face into the floor. I was dazed, my body felt weak. She slammed my head again. My vision blurred, I knew the next blow would knock me out.

"Stop!" A powerful voice yelled. It was a familiar voice I heard before.

Amy stopped, and I felt her get off of me. I looked up to see Lessia standing at the door.

Her eyes were pure white! And around her neck was the necklace with the statue hanging on it. The same one the Being had given me at Brad's house.

Lessia walked into the room and passed me. She didn't even glance at me. Her gaze was fixed on Amy. I rolled on my side, and watched amazed.

Amy backed away, as Lessia approached her. Amy stopped, and without warning leapt at Lessia. She grabbed Amy mid air and flung her back, she hit the wall and fell.

Lessia stood in front of her. Amy crouched against the wall, in fear.

"Stop doing this!" The double voice echoed from Lessia's mouth. "We need their help, have you forgotten."

Amy didn't look up, she just shook her head no. The being inside Lessia was far more powerful, that was obvious.

"You will leave that body, and never use another again!" Lessia commanded. Amy looked up, and their gazes met.

"But." Amy was about to protest. Once again she lowered her head.

"The days of revenge are gone, It was long ago." Lessia said. "The time draws close, we must prepare."

Lessia knelt in front of Amy and placed her hand on her forehead. Amy let out a ear piercing strangled cry, but did not resist. Amy fell to the floor motionless.

Lessia stood and stayed still, her back turned toward me. I saw her reach around her neck and remove the necklace. Her body swayed, and she fell to the floor, still holding the necklace.

My head started to spin, and my vision blurred. The last thing I remembered was darkness.

Opening my eyes, I looked around. Where was I?

A hospital by the look of it. I tried to move, my body was sore. Looking down, there was a cast on my left arm. And iv's in my right arm. I groaned in pain.

"Well hello there sleepy head." I heard Lessia's voice say. "How are you feeling?"

Lessia walked up to me, and touched my face softly.

"Like I have been run over by a tank." I answered, wincing in pain as I tried to move. "How long have I been here?"

"Two days," She said softly. "The doctor says you will be just fine."

She saw the shocked look on my face. She smiled at

me.

"How is Amy, is she ok did it leave." I asked, didn't know what happened after I passed out,

"Yes, it is gone and she is just fine." She said. "She doesn't remember a thing."

"And you?" I said staring into her eyes. "I saw what you did, why did you do that."

"I just knew, what I had to do." She said. "I ran downstairs, put it on and the next thing I knew. I was on the floor in Amy's room"

I told her what had happened when she came in. She was shocked, by the story.

"I have to call the base." I said. I knew I had to report for duty soon.

"I talked to your commanding officer." She said. "He said you will be helping push pencils till your better."

"Thank you." I told her. "What would I do without you.?"

"You won't ever have to worry about that." She answered with a smile.

She was silent for a moment, she leaned close and looked into my eyes.

"I love you." She said softly, touching my face.

"I love you to." I replied. I saw her eyes tear up. She kissed me softly.

The End,
Or is it?

I would like to dedicate this book to my wonderful children. Justine, Brandy, Montana and Jose jr.

Thank you to all those who stood by me, and supported me. You know who you are!!!

Chapter One
RESCUE

"Two minutes." The pilots voice said over the headphones.

The Uh-60 turned sharply, everyone inside reached out to grab anything they could. The flight of three Blackhawk helicopters skimmed low over the tops of the city buildings. As they leveled off, I saw two Apache attack helicopters join us to our right.

Looking at the soldiers in our chopper, I could see the excitement and fear in there faces.

"Ok, this is what we trained for." Brad yelled over the noise. "Let's rescue the hostages, and kill any terrorist who gets in our way. Hooah!!"

"Hooah!" all of the men responded. At the same time we pulled the charging handles on our weapons.

"One minute." The pilots voice rang out . Our helicopter slowed. Looking out the open door, I could make out the target building. There was a large fire fight in the streets. Our soldiers had surrounded the building. Bradley fighting vehicles, and M1-a2 Abrams tanks were blasting the terrorist vehicles. Burning trucks, and motionless black figures littered the streets below. Our units were advancing on the building rapidly.

The helicopter came to a stop, we hovered about 40 feet above the rooftop. Everyone waited for the command.

"Ropes!" I yelled. Quickly we grabbed the ropes, and with one quick movement repelled off the helicopter. As I leapt out, the pain in my left arm made me wince. My arm had healed well, but still hurt.

Sliding down the rope , I reached the rooftop in seconds. Letting go I took a few steps and knelt. Scanning for any targets, I held my position as the other soldiers repelled down from the Blackhawk. After all eleven of us made it down safely, we moved quickly to the door. Finding it locked the point man set a small charge. The second Blackhawk hovered overhead as the soldiers descended from it. A small but loud blast blew the metal door open, leaving it hanging on one hinge. Pushing it out of the way we entered the narrow stairway. The point man took a few steps inside and stopped. He signaled for us to do the same by raising a closed fist. Brad and I, made our way to where he was standing.

"Booby trapped, dam." Brad said shaking his head. "can you disarm it?".

The soldier knelt and examined the bomb, careful not to touch it.

"Sure, but it will take time." He said looking up at me.

"Look." Brad said pointing further down the stairs. Another explosive was positioned on the wall further down. Its small red light shined in the dim stairwell.

"We go down there and we will all be killed." I said.

"Captain, the stairs are a no go."

Brad nodded in understanding, we backed out of the stairway. Back on the roof, the third Blackhawk had just unloaded its men and was pulling away. I watched Brad's face carefully, He was in command of this operation. I was here to give advice if he asked for it.

"Shit!, the stairs were our only way down." He said shaking his head in frustration. Brad looked at me. "Any ideas Major?"

"Your in charge." I said. "Remember that Hospital in Baghdad?" It took him all but a second to recall the rescue we had done, to save trapped injured British soldiers.

A smile crossed his face. He turned and called for the squad leaders. After they were all assembled he told them the plan.

After the quick briefing, everyone lined up along the east side of the roof. With our ropes secured to a small railing, it would only be a few moments before we repelled down to began the rescue.

Brad looked at me, I nodded once and he called over the radio. The men tensed, and together we stepped off the roof and began our decent. The sound of gunfire erupted, as our troops on the ground shot out the third story windows. On the side of the building we were now descending. We would have to enter the east side, and make our way to the south west corner of the building. That is where the insurgents were holding the hostages, according to the intel we had received.

We descended rapidly down the side of the building. The snipers had done a good job shooting out the windows, it would make our entry easier.

Reaching the fourth story windows, we paused. So far we hadn't been spotted by the insurgents. I looked at the men, I could see the anticipation and fear in their faces. I called out on the headset.

"Three, two, one." I said just above a whisper. Pushing hard with my legs and releasing the rope. I swung through the broken window, and landed on the floor. Unhooking the rope, I grabbed my m-4 and scanned the large room. The first six of us knelt and aimed our weapons at the doorway, as the others swung into the room. It took only seconds for everyone to take up their positions. There was a open doorway across the room. We lined up half of us on the left side of the door, and the others on the right side.

Six men stayed behind to fasten zip lines, to be used once the rescue was complete. Bradley fighting vehicles and armored buffalos , advanced to a few feet from the building. They were to be used to transport the rescue team and hostages from the battlefield and to safety.

"Go." Brad gave the command and the first two men went through the door and into the hall. Quickly they were followed by the rest, two at a time. We proceeded through the hallway in two columns , staying as close to the walls as possible. We had found it easier for the left handed shooters to stay to the right of the hallway, and the right handed to the left. I was the third man in line on the left. Looking through my red dot sights, I could see we were coming to a intersection. Pausing the two point men entered the other hallway. We quickly followed, and were back in lines again. There were two doorways close, one on each side of the hall. As we reached them, four men did a room entry on both. Finding them empty we proceeded down the hall quickly.

Reaching the end of the long hallway we paused.

Before us was a large room with rows of chairs and a wooden desk in the front along with a large chalkboard. A empty classroom I guessed. We carefully passed through the room to the doorway on the other side. The point man knelt on one knee and raised his fist. We all knelt and pointed our weapons to the door. He made a gesture with his hands stating four enemy insurgents ahead.

Brad gave him the sign to take out the insurgents. Four men took up positions at the door two knelling and two standing. Within a split second shots rang out, even though our weapons had suppressors the sound startled us. All four men quickly went through the doorway followed by the rest of us. We went through another hallway walking in two rows. There was a set of wooden double doors with small windows at the end. The four men up front reached the doors and backed up against the walls. We stopped and Brad went quickly to where the four soldiers were standing. Using a small mirror he held it up to one of the windows. After studying the room for a quick thirty seconds he conversed with the four soldiers silently. Brad looked back at the rest of us and held out five fingers indicating the number of insurgents in the next room and pointing out their locations in the room. He then indicated eleven hostages in the room. We all tensed up and prepared ourselves for the upcoming fight. I could see the four Lead men removing flash bangs from their vests. One man pulled the door open and the other three tossed the flash bangs in.

As the men rushed the doorway, gunfire erupted

In all directions. Screams filled the room as bullets

flew. All five insurgents lay dead, as I entered the room. Gazing through the smoke filled room, I quickly did a count of our soldiers. Thank goodness only one was slightly injured, a medic already treating his wounded arm. Brad yelled for a medic as

he knelt beside a male hostage who was bleeding from his shoulder. Brad stood and gave the order to evacuate the hostages back to the waiting vehicles.

The soldiers helped the stunned hostages to their feet and began heading back.

"They took the ambassador to a room at the end of the hall just before you got here." A woman said as she pointed down a hallway. Brad called out for A squad to follow him. I quickly stepped forward and joined them. Brad told his L.T. to evacuate everyone back to the vehicles and we would go get the ambassador and meet up with them shortly.

"If we are not back in twenty minutes, give us another twenty minutes." Brad told the L.T. with a big grin. The L.T. gave Brad a pat on the shoulder and quickly left. A squad formed up and we headed down the hallway the woman had pointed at.

The hallway was not very long and at the end was a single door. Being so close to the area of the firefight we knew whomever was in there would be ready for us. Quietly reaching the door we took our positions for a room entry. The man on point kicked the door hard, as it swung open the others entered the room.

"Drop your weapon." I heard a soldier yell as I entered. Behind a large wooden desk stood a black clad insurgent holding a pistol to the head of a middle aged man who was shaking in fear.

"No you drop your weapons," the insurgent said in a calm voice. "I am not afraid to die, so I will take him with me if you don't back away." His voice was strangely calm, without a hint of fear. We all stood unmoving weapons pointing directly at him. His gaze went slowly around the room, pausing for a second on each soldier. As he made eye contact with me, I felt a strange chill, something very familiar but I couldn't place it. As I looked into his eyes my heart froze. For a split second I saw his eyes change, from a dark brown to pure white! I have encountered those eyes before but how could this be? And why here why now? A sly smile lit up his face as he stared at me.

"I know you." He spoke softly. A strange double voice, a voice I was all to familiar with. He leaned as if to get closer. A loud crack filled the room, glass flying in all directions. Within the span of a heartbeat his head exploded in a cloud of grey matter and bone fragments. Blood sprayed the soldiers next to me. His nearly headless body dropped to the floor with a thud.

"Target eliminated." Came a voice over the radio. So

caught up in the mans gaze I failed to notice the hovering helicopter outside the window. The sniper had done his job with precision, waiting for the perfect opportunity before taking the shot. One of the soldiers ran forward and helped the shaken ambassador to his feet.

"Are you hit?" the soldier asked. The man shook his head in the negative. I walked over to the body and with my foot turned it over. On its neck he wore a necklace with a small wooden angel. I knelt down swiftly and with my gloved hand ripped it from his neck and carefully placed it in one of the pockets of my vest.

"Lets go." Brad said as he headed to the door. Everyone followed and we rapidly made our way back to our exit. Waiting for our turn on the zip lines I reached into my vest removing the necklace, I showed it to Brad. His eyes opened wide with a look of shock. We were next so I quickly put the necklace back in my vest and put the clamp on the rope and slid down to the waiting vehicles. As we drove away I was thankful for a successful mission. One man with a minor wound, and a hostage that would recover quickly from his wound. Brad had done an excellent job. He was well respected by his men and a fine officer. During the bumpy ride back, my mind was filled with the insurgents eyes, voice and what he said before he was killed. How did he know me? The answer showed itself the second I saw the necklace.

Home

As I walked quickly through the airport terminal. I scanned the faces in the crowed. I had let Lessia know that my plane would be landing at 6:00 pm. I couldn't wait to see her, I had missed her so much during my three month deployment. Now that Brad was in charge of the unit, I wouldn't have to leave very often. It would be nice just to spend all our time together. Besides I am getting to old for this, let the younger men have their time.

I heard a woman's scream as I turned a corner. A beautiful woman with long black hair was running at me. She had tears in her eyes yet the biggest smile I had ever seen. Within a second she reached me and leapt into my arms. Lessa buried her face in my chest and between sobs said how much she missed me and loved me. I held her tight and for a long moment we stood still. While people in the crowd passed us with smiles and a man even patted my shoulder as he passed. Slowly Lessa put her feet on the ground but didn't stop her embrace. She lifted her head and with tear filled eyes she said how glad she was I was home. I told her I missed her so much and how I thought of her every moment, she smiled and put her arm around my waist as we began to leave.

Once outside she stiffened and stopped walking.

"Where did you get that statue?" She said with a hint of sadness in her voice. I never told her anything about it, she must have just sensed it.

Would you believe I got it off a dead insurgent." I said

"His eyes and voice was the same as the others, and he told me he knew me right before he was killed." Lessa just shook her head. "Those things are just popping up everywhere." She said. She again put her arm around me and we continued walking through the parking area.

"I brought the BMW I figured you would want to drive home." She said with a giggle.

"How did you know?" I joked. I had gotten used to her abilities, she knew me better than I knew myself.

I had thought about how I would propose to her. But I knew she would know before I asked, So I would have to find a way to surprise her. Lessa nudged me with her shoulder, as I looked at her she gave me a sly smile and winked. I just laughed, it would be a challenge.

We got to my grey BMW and she gave me the keys.

I through my pack in the trunk and smiled from ear to ear as I started the engine. I loved this car, but also missed the eclipse. But unfortunately it couldn't be fixed and had to be retired to the great junkyard in the sky. As we drove home I asked her if she wanted to stop somewhere for dinner. Never letting go of me she said she was planning to make me a home cooked meal. I replied by stepping on the gas to hurry home which made her laugh,

After arriving home Lessa told me to go take a long hot shower. To get the sand out of my hair she joked, she would make dinner in the mean time. The hot water from the shower felt so refreshing, just what I needed. It had been three months since I was able to say I felt clean. Putting on jeans and a tee shirt I headed down stairs. The aroma of real food hit me as I reached the bottom of the stairs. A long hot shower, regular clothes and Lessa's wonderful cooking. Now that's worth coming home too. As we ate she filled me in on all the family news. Her family had just opened a second restaurant in the city. She said since the road sign went up at the original café, business was booming. And they finally had the money for a second place. Their goal had always been to open up a chain of cafes, now it was coming true. She also told me my

Kids had visited her often, even taking her out to eat. I was so happy to hear that, they had been getting close over the past months and it made everything go smoothly. She told me she had spent a lot of time helping her family set up the new café, that way her mind was busy. This deployment was hard on her but between being with the kids and her family she was able to cope.

She was so happy to hear that Brad had officially taken over the unit and my deployment days were over. I explained to her how the deployment went and how the mission was a complete success. We talked for what seemed like hours about everything. She gave me a slight smile and told me its time for bed. Taking my hand she led me quickly upstairs.

I stirred in bed, I must have had a bad dream. Sitting up I felt a little uneasy. Lessa was already up, she wasn't n bed plus I could smell fresh coffee. Throwing on some clothes I went downstairs. Entering the kitchen Lessa was busy making breakfast which smelled great. Upon seeing me she smiled and came up and gave me a kiss.

"Good morning sleepy head." She teased. I smiled and gave her a hug.

"How did you sleep?" I asked her. letting go of her I headed to the coffee pot.

"With you holding me I slept better than I have in months." She replied with a smile. "The kids said they would be by soon to visit"

"That will be amazing, I cant wait to see them" I replied. Taking a big gulp of coffee I went outside to the back porch for a cigarette. After each deployment it always took me a few days to adjust back to a normal life. Sometimes it felt like I lived in two separate lives. But my life now will start to normalize, no more deployments. After the twenty days of leave I will be at the base nearby to train and consult. I will miss the action of the missions, but now I can enjoy all the things people take for granted. I am getting up there in years and keeping up with the younger soldiers was beginning to become difficult.

"Babe, breakfast is ready." Lessa said gently. She knew I was deep in thought and didn't want to startle me. I followed her inside and together we enjoyed breakfast. We had a busy but fun day, being with the kids and Lessa showed me that my life was going better than I could have imagined.

After being out all day we parted and with many hugs the kids headed home, I always missed not being with them all day every day, but I hoped that I was showing them just how important they are to me.

Lessa and I sat at the kitchen table drinking iced coffee when the doorbell rang. Lessa looked worried, the smile on her face vanished. As I got up to go answer the door she followed me grabbing my arm for comfort. I opened the door and froze, I heard Lessa gasp softly.

"Father Clarence, what a surprise come in." I said nervous. I waved him in and led him to the sofa. He gave a quick glance of his surroundings before sitting down." Would you like anything, coffee, tea?" Lessa asked. "Coffee would be great, black please." He answered. Lessa quickly went into the kitchen.

"So what's going on, if you traveled here I assume something bad has happened?" I asked.

"Yes I am in need of your help, He said fidgeting. Lessa came back in to the room and handed the Father a steaming coffee. He continued to tell us of a small boy that was showing the same symptoms as the girl in our last encounter. He admitted that alone he felt he would not be able to help the boy. He admitted that during the last encounter he felt he failed to really help the girl. Lessa asked the proper questions and Father Clarence told us it had started about four days ago for the boy. The parents were at a loss on how to help their son. The doctors they took him to said there was nothing wrong with him physically. And recommended to have the child get mental help. So they went to talk with the priest first, who contacted Father Clarence.

"Have you seen the boy yet?" Lessa asked. "Oh yes, its some much different than the last one." He stated. He told us that prayer, holy objects and even holy water had no effect on him. Lessa and I exchanged knowing glances.

"Father I know what is affecting the boy, its not actually evil. It's the same kind of being I encountered at my friends home. It had possessed his daughter." I continued. "Nothing would affect it, holy water did nothing to it , and not even Father Patrick could help."

The father nodded his head and made the sign of the cross for respect of his friend. Everyone in the room was quiet for a moment. "So what do you suggest.?" The Father asked.

"Find out its intentions and just have a discussion with it, there is really nothing that can be done that will make it leave the boys body." I said truthfully.

"We cant just do nothing." Lessa said "Lets go see the boy and figure out what this thing wants and convince it to leave the boy alone." The Father looked hopefully to Lessa and then to me.

I sat quiet, thinking about what could be done. The last encounter had nearly killed me. The encounter with Brads daughter was far less physically dangerous, but that being was by far more powerful. It had just wanted to talk. Could this being now be the same? Lessa was right, we wouldn't know until we confronted it face to face.

"Your right Lessa." I said. "We need to meet the boy and see exactly what its intentions are. Then maybe we can find a way to help."

Both their faces lit up, Father Clarence gave me a smile followed by a nod. Lessa made a fist and said yess!! I couldn't help but be lifted by her attitude. The Father after giving us the address, happily shook our hands and told us he would wait for us to arrive there before continuing anything. He left the house in a far better mood than he came.

Lessa smiled and headed upstairs to grab a few things.

The directions the Father gave us were only about sixty miles away. We ended up taking Lessa's jeep grand Cherokee it had a lot more room to take things with us. As we left the city, I sat in the passenger seat and began wondering if this had anything to do with the necklace the insurgent was wearing when he was killed. Both Lessa and I had carefully taken it out of my pack and locked it up with the other two. It seemed trouble always surfaced when we came into contact with them.

Its just down the next street Lessa said. She slowed down and we almost idled to the house. Pulling into the curb

She shut the engine off, we were parked right behind Father Clarence's car. Lessa was silent for awhile just staring at the house.

"This is going to be bad." She said above a whisper. "What's wrong, what do you feel?" I asked her. "I cant be sure, but I think it may be the same entity you encountered at Brads house. She said. "It wont be so bad that entity didn't harm me," I said hopeful.

"Don't be hopeful, It seems really angry." She said. She kept staring at the house, I could see the concern on her face. Let's go inside she said. We got out and walked to the door.

Father Clarence opened the door as I held my hand up to knock, startling us. He had a serious expression on his face. After telling us to come in we were seated on the couch.

"The boy is currently sleeping, his mother is with him." He said. "I tried to converse with the entity, like you had mentioned. But it told me the one it wanted to talk to would arrive shortly."

I looked at Lessa but her gaze was fixed to the dark hallway. She had a blank expression on her face. Her eyes squinted as if sensing something.

"What do you feel?" I asked her. She seemed to snap back to reality. Turning to me she spoke softly.

"I think it wants you, the feeling I am getting is it took over the boy just to get you here." She said "Apparently you have unfinished business with it."

"What?, What could it want.?" I said shocked. "Lessa you were the last one to encounter it. You put the necklace on when you confronted the Nephilim. Did you sense anything then?"

"No once I put it on everything went blank, I don't

Remember a thing after that" she said." I remember waking up on the floor near you."

"Ok now we know this thing doesn't want the boy, so I figure it will let him go once it completes its business with me." I said.

"More than likely." Father Clarence stated. "This is very unsettling, this is a spiritual matter of which the church has no power, but if you don't mind I would like to be present till the end."

"Of course Father, your assistance will be greatly welcomed and needed." Lessa told him. The Father shook his head. Happy to know he still had a role in the up coming events.

The wait was nerve racking. Father Clarence and Lessa were discussing her abilities. While I played the meeting with the entity over and over in my head thinking what it could want from me. Lessa had mentioned that it was angry. Angry about what I wondered. What had I done to upset it? My last mission I thought. The insurgent that was killed was wearing a necklace also. Could his death have upset it?

It was not good to have all these thoughts running through my head. I was just confusing myself more. Once the boy wakes, all my questions will be answered I thought. About four hours passed, all the conversations died down. Father Clarence was the first to fall asleep. He was seated on a grey recliner snoring softly. I was sitting on the end of the matching sofa, and Lessa was curled up beside me with her head on my lap sleeping soundly. I was both in and out of sleep. Feeling restless and unable to mover for fear of waking Lessa.

In the back of my mind I could hear footsteps. Opening my eyes, I saw a woman coming down the dark hallway. With a startled look she stopped when she saw me.

"Who are you?" The woman said, looking at me. "Are you the ones the Father called?"

"Yes, Father Clarence had us come. My name is Jose." I said. The sound of my voice woke Lessa who sat up rubbing her eyes. Father Clarence opened his eyes and began to stretch.

"Im Rita, Im Carlos's mom. When did you get here?" She asked.

"Last night, the Father did not want us to disturb you. So he said we would wait for you." I answered.

"Hello Lessa said politely." She got up from the sofa and walked over to shake her hand. She introduced herself with a smile. Rita seemed to relax now that she knew who we were. Father Clarence got up and walked over to her, Putting his arm around her he led her to the kitchen and sat her on one of the four chairs. He turned on the kurig and made her a cup of coffee. He asked her how things had gone last night.

She told him that Carlos had slept the whole time and was still sleeping when she left the room. The Father smiled and patted her arm. He told her everything would be fine, He then called Lessa and I over and told us to sit down.

We talked with Rita about how it all started. She told us at first he withdrew from everyone just staying in his room. He told his parents he was very tired and wasn't feeling well. When asked where the pain was he couldn't say. So as worried parents they took him to see a doctor. After running a few tests, everything came back normal. He said he was feeling a lot better even though no treatment was given. So they discharged him and recommended he make an appointment at the nearby mental health clinic, After arriving home he went straight to his room and went to sleep. When he awoke that night his behavior had changed. He was mean with his parents, even pushing them away if they got to close to him. His voice changed to a double voice one seeming a lot lower and menacing. When his eyes changed from brown to pure white it set them into a panic. Carlos started demanding to see a priest and even threatened his parents if they would not comply. They went to the local church and the priest agreed to come see him. After the priest had left he called Father Clarence to come by quickly. When he arrived Carlos told him to get a hold of you two or the entity would start harming Carlos and the parents. So here we all are she said looking at us.

"I admit this case doesn't fit the guidelines the church has set up for situations like this. The lack of reaction to holy objects would disqualify this case in the eyes of the church." Father Clarence said. "But I know in my heart that this is a true possession by an actual spiritual entity, so I am going to see it through."

"Thank you so much for helping my son." Rita thanked the Father.

Lessa suddenly got up and faced the hallway. A second after a loud crash echoed down the hall shaking the house. "He's awake and not very happy." she whispered. The hair stood up on my neck as I knew bad things were going to happen. The tree of us stood up and joined Lessa, following her as she walked down the hallway.

Reaching the room Father Clarence put his hand on the doorknob. I took position behind him and stood protectively in front of Lessa. Opening the door we walked in. A large dresser lay in pieces on the floor next to the twin bed. The boy was sitting on the middle of the bed. He seemed about eleven years old I would have guessed. A slight build for his age and the same light brown hair as his mothers. But what unnerved me the most was his pure white eyes. He just sat there staring directly at me. Everyone gathered around the bed. The boy didn't move. He didn't seem to notice everyone else, just continued to look into my eyes.

"You killed him." The boy spoke with a familiar eerie double voice. "I told you to make it known the end was coming, and how to stop it. But you didn't."

"Who would listen to me.?" I said quietly. I remembered what it had told me during our first encounter. The thought struck me that this was the same entity that had taken over Brads daughter Brandi.

"I found someone who was in the position and willing to listen, and you killed him before he could spread the warning to those that matter." It continued.

"It appears that by just telling you that you did not understand the urgency of the situation."

The boy reached out his hand showing a small wooden angel in his palm. I cringed at the sight of it. Wherever those idols were trouble would soon follow.

The boy whispered something but I wasn't able to hear. I took a step closer.

"Since you didn't listen, I will have to show you!" The voice growled. Within a split second the boy leapt from the bed and wrapped his arms around me. I suddenly felt a horrible sense of nausea overtake me. I felt a sharp sting on the back of my neck, Weakened I fell onto the bed still in the boys grasp. A deep darkness settled in, like someone was dimming the light. I heard a woman scream, I think it was Lessa but it faded fast. A strange sensation enveloped me, like falling in the dark. The last thing I saw was two bright points that seemed to shrink. I realized in that instant those were my eyes that the light was coming through. As they faded in the distance there was nothing but a horrible blackness that remained.

Before Lessa could even react the boy leapt from the bed without warning and jumped Jose who had for some reason moved closer to the bed.

The boy let go and started yelling for his mom. She quickly ran from the door and hugged him tight. He was crying and appeared to not know what had happened.

Rita took him out of the room. Father Clarence seemed to be in a state of confusion. Lessa turned Jose's motionless body over. She gasped, his eyes were open and instead of his blue eyes there were pure white eyes. No! she thought this cant be happening. She franticly searched around for the wooden idol. She spotted it by his neck and slapped it away. She shook him several times calling out his name. There was no response. Lessa stood up taking a deep breath she needed to get herself under control. She needed to be calm if she was going to sense anything and be of any help. She closed her eyes and took another deep breath. It's not going to hurt him is the feeling she got, It is going to show him something. But how long will all this take? She thought. I am going to need help. I cant sense him anymore she thought. She started to panic.

"I'm going to call for help so we can take him to the church, there is a spare room where we can keep him." Father Clarence said. Lessa nodded in understanding. He left the room to make the call and check on the boy.

Lessa stood at the foot of the bed with her eyes closed. She was hoping to get a feeling of what happened. She couldn't sense anything no entity or Jose. She was starting to get frightened, Usually she could feel something. Wherever they are she cant sense them. I don't know what to do she thought I need help. Opening her eyes she looked around for his phone. Not seeing it on the bed she searched his pockets. Finding it she Pulled it out and swiped the screen. She knew it wasn't locked, he always said she was free to go through it. She laughed to herself, she trusted him completely she would sense if he was hiding anything from her. She even knew he wanted to propose to her, but was waiting to surprise her. That wouldn't happen she would feel it coming before he had a chance to pop the question. Looking through his contacts she found the person she was looking for she hit call.

"Hey Major what's up?" Brad said as he answered his phone. He was surprised to see the majors number pop up. "Lessa, whats wrong is everything ok?" He could hear the fear in her voice.

He tried to calm her down so she could speak clearly. Lessa explained to him everything that had happened.

There was a moment of silence

As he tried to absorb what was going on. Sure I will get a plane ticket and be there as soon as I can. Megan had overheard the conversation and told Brad and Lessa she was going also. She would call her mom to watch Brandi while they were gone. Brandi also heard the conversation and told her mom she was going with them. Brad and Megan fell silent. No way are you going they sternly told Brandi.

"Mom, Dad I remember everything that happened to me." She told them. "It started coming back to me a few weeks after it happened. I didn't say anything to you because I thought you would have me go through therapy or something."

"You should have said something." Megan scolded. But before she could continue Brandi interrupted.

"I have been there, right now he is in a cold dark place. I can help him to find hid way out." She said.

Brad and Megan looked at each other. Finally Brad shrugged his shoulders. With a sigh Megan told her to go pack a small bag with necessities only. Brandi excitedly ran up the stairs to pack. Hearing the conversation over the phone even Lessa said it was a good idea that Brandi could help.

"Well I will get three tickets for the first flight out." He told Lessa.

Thank goodness she thought as she hung up the phone. She placed it in her back pocket. Just then Father Clarence returned to the room. Two men accompanied him. By the look of their clothes they had to be fellow priests. Between the four of them they struggled to get Jose out of the house to an awaiting suv. Once he was safely inside they informed the two priests that they would follow in their own vehicles. The two men nodded and got in the vehicle. Father Clarence got in his car, and with one last look at the house Lessa got in her Jeep. At least the boy is safe and out of danger she thought to herself before starting the engine.

Darkness total and ultimate darkness. Absolutely no sensation whatsoever. No sound no light no feeling. I try to talk but there is no sound. I try to move but there is nothing. A feeling of panic sets in. Suddenly I sence something. Not by sound or touch but by knowing something is there, Whatever it is, is trying to tell me something. There is no sound, I just know its trying to talk with me. What's going on I think to myself. "I brought you hear", not a voice but more like a thought. "Just think what you want to say". I understand now that's how you communicate through thoughts." Yes" came the response. "Who are you?" I thought. "Surely you remember me." Was the response.

"I brought you here to show you what I told you earlier" it responded. "Since you did not head my words, I wanted you to see and understand what is facing us all."

"How can I see? I replied. I couldn't see a thing in this blackness.

"You are energy, you don't have sight touch or sound as you know it." came the response." I will merge with you for a moment and you will understand."

Not knowing what to expect I felt fear. Instead there was disorientation. When I realized what happened I was in a unfamiliar room. The colors we off, like seeing things through a strange filter. I could make out the shapes of three people in the room. The figures were dark but around each of then was a grayish glow. On a bed was another figure but without the glow surrounding it. I wanted to walk over and see who it was but I couldn't move." Just think it" It responded. Following what it said I was instantly next to the bed. To move I only had to think it. Everything was so strange. I was in this room but could not feel a thing. There was no hot or cold no feeling of the movement of air on my skin as I moved. Looking at myself I could dimly make out a figure of myself. But around my figure there was also a grayish glow. I don't understand I thought to myself.

"The aura you sense is energy, The energy given to your kind by the creator." It responded. Beside me there was a brighter glow, but with no figure in the center. "I was never born as a human so I have no form. I am pure energy."

"I understand." I replied. " Humans had both a physical form and a spiritual form combined".

"Yes." it responded. "Your kind are the only ones in the universe to have both. Remember what I told you before. The creator joined both together in the hope that we could have a body. But the fleshly part of your bodies corrupt us and we are no longer pure."

"I do remember what you told me. But experiencing it firsthand is very different." I thought. Looking down at the figure laying on the bed shocked me. It was myself laying there but there was no glow around my body.

"You are not in your body at the moment. You are here." It responded. "Your body is not dead I am keeping it alive till you return to it."

I thought of the other three figures in the room, and instantly I was beside them. One was Father Clarence and the other I did not know. The third was Lessa. I wanted to touch her, but did not know how so I tried to think it. There was no feeling as I passed right through her. I tried talking to her but couldn't. To them I was non existent.

"That is one reason we had the idols created. As a way for us to communicate with you." It responded.

"Ok so what did you want to show me.?" I questioned the entity. Hoping to hurry this along.

"What one of us knows we all know." It stated. "I will show you now."

Images flashed before me at an incredible rate. A blue sun exploding filling the void with light and matter. As it cooled stars and planets and whole galaxy's were formed out of the dust and ash. A long journey lasting for a billion years before finding life. A race of strange creatures remotely human like in appearance. But reproduction was to slow for the vast number needed. So the search went on, Earth the same but different, Man was just starting to settle into small groups. The creator attempted to join with them to form a dual being. But the savage ways of the early humans made those who come in contact with them unpure. Even the glow emitted by them dulled from a bright dazzling white light to a dull grey. The creator feared they would infect the rest of them. He wanted to destroy the humans and those whom they infected, But was unable. He communicated with the beings he first encountered and offered them Earth if they would kill every last human. They traveled space in a huge craft to earth. But being vastly outnumbered they were forced to leave Earth. They returned to their home world. Losing most of their numbers in the war with earth. Their race was on the verge of extinction.

Some returned to earth to secretly test the possibility of using human women as surrogates of their embryos. A sure way to avoid the extinction they faced. Being successful in their experiments. They hid their ship in the ocean depths where it wouldn't be discovered. And they would kidnap a thousand human women a year to become surrogates for their children, During the birth process the human women would not survive, their bodies be disposed of in the crushing ocean depts. The creator told them that humans must never leave the planet or their race and others would be in danger. So they devised a plan to eliminate all human life on the surface. But they wait till humans are about to leave the planet before putting their plan into action. Every year they wait, makes their race a thousand stronger.

The creator will wait because tim has no meaning to him, But once the humans are all destroyed he and those he created will come back to Earth and will end all the fallen beings of his kind and lure all the human spirits to where he can destroy them totally. Ending once and for all the human mistake he created.

But there is a flaw in his plan. One way to stop

All his plans from happening. That is the message this Being has been trying to get across to humans. If the ship hiding in the ocean can be destroyed. Then the attack will be stopped. And since the creator can not destroy the humans himself. He would be forced to abandon his plan. Both the human race and all the spiritual beings would be safe and flourish.

"Now you see, I have shown you what you needed to know." It responded. "Now is your time to tell those who have the power to stop them."

A familiar voice called my name. It started as a distant eco but was growing steadily louder.

Lessa and Brandi sat on each side of the bed, holding his hands they watched the still body for and reaction or movement. Brad paced around the room as Father Clarence and Megan sat on chairs in the corner.

"Jose if you can hear me follow my voice." Brandi repeated. She had been holding his hand for a half hour calling out to him. She understood the dark place he was in. She had been there herself.

"Do you sense anything?" Brad asked Lessa for the twentieth time. He was beginning to worry he wouldn't come out of this. Lessa took a slow breath and closed her eyes trying to be open to any sign. She could have sworn earlier she had felt him near her. While she was talking to the priests. It was only a fleeting sensation. She told Brad when they had arrived and Brandi seemed optimistic.

"Jose can you hear me come to my voice." Brandi repeated. She gave his hand a hard squeeze. She was about to repeat it when Lessa gave a loud sob.

Brandi looked up at her and at the same moment she felt her hand being squeezed. "Jose are you there, can you hear me." She said hopefully. Again she felt him squeeze her had. Lessa was crying no "I sense him." Was all she could say.

"Follow my voice." Brandi said louder. "Look his eyes!" everyone was on their feet and moved closer to the bed. His eyes were no longer white but the light blue they had all remembered

I heard voices. I could actually hear voices in the darkness. Ahead of me were two pinpoints of light. I thought of them and they rapidly grew larger. Reaching the lights I could see a roof and worried faces through them. I realized I was looking through my eyes. I could feel the warmth of hands holding mine, and the sounds of people talking. I could feel the lumpy bed underneath me.

Lessa put her head to his chest and cried as he started to stir. Brandi gave a wide smile as Jose began blinking his eyes and looking around the room.

Brad breathed a deep sigh of relief as he fought to hold back tears of his own. Father Clarence made the sigh of the cross and said a silent prayer. Megan put her arms around Brad as he began to softly cry.

Lessa to wrapped up in her emotions, heard Jose whisper something. She raised her head and looked into his eyes. Again she heard him whisper.

"Lessa will you marry me?" Jose whispered. Slowly he

reached into his pocket and pulled out a golden engagement ring.

"What?" Lessa replied in shock. "Yes of course." she stammered caught totally by surprise. You had me so damn worried." she scolded him as he put the ring on her finger. She looked into his eyes and her voice softened. "Yes," she whispered and gave him a kiss.

Three Days Later

I heard Lessa's jeep pull into the driveway as I was having a cup of coffee at the table. She walked through the front door, A big smile on her face. She walked up to me and gave me a kiss.

"There are so many things to do before the wedding." She said happily. "Megan and Brandi will be coming this weekend. And my mom and my sister will be here also. We have to get fitted for the dresses in person."

I gave her a big smile. I was hoping to catch her by surprise again.

"Sit down." I told her "I have something for you." I watched the surprise on her face as she sat down." now close your eyes and reach out your hand." She closed her eye tight and held out her hand. I pulled out an envelope I had hidden on my lap and placed it in her hand. "Now open your eyes."

She opened her eyes and studied the blank envelope, Opening it she read the papers inside.

I heard her gasp, "Our honeymoon in Rome! " she could barely speak. "Oh my god thank you." she got up and jumped on my lap. Hugging me tight I knew it was a great day. That's twice I had managed to surprise he with something. "I cant wait to tell my mom and sister." She said. Giving me another tight hug and a long kiss. She got up grabbing her phone from the table she made the call. "Mom, you will never guess where we are going on our honeymoon." She said the excitement evident in her voice.

I took another sip of coffee with a smile.

The End,
Or is it?

www.ingramcontent.com/pod-product-compliance
Lightning Source LLC
Chambersburg PA
CBHW030258130626
46549CB00002B/583